# Equity Doesn't Just Happen

# Equity Doesn't Just Happen

## Stories of Education Leaders Working toward Social Justice

*Edited by*

Jo Smith
Elisabeth Crowell Kim

ROWMAN & LITTLEFIELD
*Lanham • Boulder • New York • London*

Published by Rowman & Littlefield
An imprint of The Rowman & Littlefield Publishing Group, Inc.
4501 Forbes Boulevard, Suite 200, Lanham, Maryland 20706
www.rowman.com

86-90 Paul Street, London EC2A 4NE, United Kingdom

Copyright © 2023 by Jo Smith and Elisabeth Crowell Kim

*All rights reserved.* No part of this book may be reproduced in any form or by any electronic or mechanical means, including information storage and retrieval systems, without written permission from the publisher, except by a reviewer who may quote passages in a review.

British Library Cataloguing in Publication Information Available

**Library of Congress Cataloging-in-Publication Data**

Names: Smith, Joanna, 1974- editor. | Kim, Elisabeth Crowell, 1977- editor.
Title: Equity doesn't just happen : stories of education leaders working toward social justice / edited by Joanna Smith, Elisabeth Crowell Kim.
Description: Lanham, Maryland : Rowman & Littlefield, 2023. | Includes bibliographical references and index. | Summary: "This volume offers a mix of theory and application on equity work in schools, districts, and states."—Provided by publisher.
Identifiers: LCCN 2022039419 (print) | LCCN 2022039420 (ebook) | ISBN 9781475865387 (cloth) | ISBN 9781475865394 (paperback) | ISBN 9781475865400 (epub)
Subjects: LCSH: Educational leadership—Social aspects. | Social justice and education. | Culturally relevant pedagogy.
Classification: LCC LB2806 .E78 2023 (print) | LCC LB2806 (ebook) | DDC 371.2/011—dc23/eng/20220930
LC record available at https://lccn.loc.gov/2022039419
LC ebook record available at https://lccn.loc.gov/2022039420

# Contents

Foreword: Equity Doesn't Just Happen: Stories of Education
    Leaders Working Toward Social Justice     vii
    *Decoteau J. Irby, University of Illinois, Chicago*

Acknowledgments     ix

Introduction     xi
    *Jo Smith, University of Auckland, New Zealand*

Chapter 1: Motivations and Mechanisms: Stories of Education
    Leadership Pathways     1
    *Elisabeth Crowell Kim, California State University, Monterey Bay*

Chapter 2: Enacting Culturally Responsive School Leadership:
    Experiences Working Toward Institutional Change     15
    *Iton Udosenata, Salem-Keizer Public Schools, Oregon*

Chapter 3: Culturally Sustaining and Socially Just Leadership
    Practice: Engaging in Collaborative Equity Audits     25
    *George Theoharis, Syracuse University; Christine A. Ashby, Syracuse University; Sarah Gentile, West Genesee Central School District; Nate Franz, Jamesville-DeWitt School District; Corey Williams, Syracuse City School District; Benjamin Steuerwalt, Syracuse City School District; Rory Edwards, Syracuse City School District; and Meredith Devennie, Liverpool Central School District*

Chapter 4: Flipping the Script through Virtual Reality
    Perspective-Taking to Increase the Culture of Belonging     39
    *Wendy Morgan, SHIFT, and Heather McClure, University of Oregon's Center for Education Promotion*

Chapter 5: Equity in Action: Efforts and Challenges of Recruiting and Retaining Teachers and Leaders of Color in Our Schools and Districts  49
*Gustavo Balderas, Beaverton School District, Oregon*

Chapter 6: Culturally Responsive and Socially Just Leadership Practice: Creating Inclusive Service Delivery  67
*George Theoharis, Syracuse University, Sarah D. Lent, Wisconsin Center of Education Research, and Kimana Kibriani, Syracuse University*

Chapter 7: Tribe–School District Relationships for Policy Change toward Social Justice  83
*Mona Halcomb, Washington Office of Superintendent of Public Instruction*

Chapter 8: Challenging Leadership to Meet the Needs of Muslim Students in New Zealand  95
*Deborah J. Lomax, Cognition Education Group*

Index  111

Contributors  113

# Foreword

## *Equity Doesn't Just Happen: Stories of Education Leaders Working Toward Social Justice*

Decoteau J. Irby, University of Illinois, Chicago

I started my education career in Philadelphia where I taught adjudicated 15 to 21 year-olds to take and pass the General Equivalency Degree test as part of a life skills program. At age 23 I wasn't much older than my students, who were all Black and attended the program as a court-ordered condition of their probation. After a rocky start, I learned quickly that meeting the needs of my students required understanding who they were and creating learning opportunities that drew on their interests while preparing them for a better future. I showed up to work each day working to challenge the ways that traditional schools had failed to meet my students' learning and socio-emotional needs.

Twenty years later I continue to advocate for educators to create and maintain learning conditions and opportunities that will serve our society's most vulnerable youth. But now I do so from the position of a university professor, author, and activist. In my university teaching, I prepare school leaders to work in schools with students who share similar life and educational experiences and who come from communities and homes that remain remarkably similar to those I encountered in Philadelphia: economically and politically underserved and disenfranchised; pathologized and chastised by mainstream society as inherently problematic and irredeemable just for being poor or different; and despite these realities, filled with potential and aspiration.

My commitment as an author and activist is to ensure school-based educators are prepared and willing to establish learning conditions and practices that accept students for who they are while also nourishing the seeds of who they are constantly becoming. In this volume, Drs. Jo Smith and Elisabeth Kim leverage their years of research and teaching to advance this cause. With chapter contributions from early-career and established educational researchers and practitioners, this book's strength is its balance of personal narrative and practical guidance.

Placing personal narratives and practical guidance in the same volume conveys that enacting equity-based and social justice–oriented leadership approaches is often deeply personal. The stories of *why* leaders might take these approaches are important because numbers alone are inadequate to compel change and action in the service of marginalized children and youth. Indeed, if decades of evidence that demonstrate the pressing need for educators to adopt thesep approaches were adequate, the associated practices would be more widely used.

For readers who want to better serve students and communities that for decades have experienced marginalization in schools, *Equity Doesn't Just Happen: Stories of Education Leaders Working Toward Social Justice* offers straightforward accounts of how and why these approaches benefit hiring and retention, inclusion education, and much more. Ultimately what readers stand to gain is an understanding of how to keep children and young people in school, engaged, and inspired. If educators were equipped with volumes such as this to learn from, perhaps we might do better at helping our students' potential and aspiration blossom into promising futures.

*Decoteau J. Irby is an associate professor at University of Illinois at Chicago and author of* Stuck Improving: Racial Equity and School Leadership *and* Magical Black Tears: A Protest Story.

# Acknowledgments

First and foremost, we'd like to thank Penny Wohlstetter, our mentor, guide, and ultimately the inspiration for this work. Penny was the principal investigator of the Diverse by Design charter schools project that sparked the initial discussion of honoring the voices of leaders engaged in equity work, highlighting their motivations as well as the mechanisms that propelled them on their leadership journeys. We are grateful to have had the opportunity to work with Penny on this project, spanning 28 campuses in five cities in three states. This project would not have been possible without an excellent supportive team of researchers, and so we thank Sarah Cordes, Brandon Harrington, Elizabeth Huffaker, Josh Ingram, Sakshi Jain, Bren Kleinfelder, Lorna Porter, and Sophia Seifert. Similarly we'd like to thank the leaders in those schools who gave so graciously of their time to share their experiences not just in their current leadership positions but everything leading up to it, often starting with a formative experience from their childhood. They are truly striving to live their values of equity-minded, social justice–oriented leadership.

Next we'd like to thank the contributing authors who shared such vibrant chapters on efforts to increase and enact social justice–oriented leadership. This book started on a virtual panel at the American Educational Research Association (AERA) Annual Meeting in 2021. We were inspired by the work of our co-presenters George Theoharis, Sarah Lent, Christine Ashby, and Kimana Kibriani as well as members of the Syracuse City, West Genesee, Jamesville-Dewitt Central, and Liverpool School Districts in upstate New York including Sarah Gentile, Nate Franz, Corey Williams, Benjamin Steuerwalt, Rory Edwards, and Meredith Devennie. We are so pleased that this project has come to fruition from that initial AERA session. Another chance meeting—this one during a symposium on experiences with culturally responsive education in New Zealand and Malaysia—resulted in the chapter by Deborah Lomax focused on Muslim students in New Zealand, showcasing that equity work spans continents, culture, and context.

We also offer our gratitude and awe to the education leaders working in Oregon and Washington who contributed such critical perspectives to this volume. The three chapters authored by Gustavo Balderas, Mona Halcomb, and Iton Udosenata show how leadership theory translates into leadership-in-practice. Their lived experiences—the victories as well as the setbacks—provide glimmers of hope, optimism, and strength in combating bias and striving for true equity. Sincere thanks also to Heather McClure and Wendy Morgan for their fascinating contribution describing the potential of virtual reality to increase empathy in efforts to foster a sense of belonging in schools. Finally we'd like to thank Decoteau Irby for contributing the foreword to this volume. His ideas tie this volume together superbly.

On a personal note, we are grateful to our families for their support. Betsy would like to thank her husband, Howie, and kids, Elise and Hal, as well as her Uncle Steve and Aunt Kathy, who always believed in her and did everything they could to help her reach her goals. Jo would like to thank her partner, David, and her colleagues and students from her adopted home of Auckland, where she continues to be humbled by the teachings offered by her new environs and grateful to be invited to share learnings from her time in the Pacific Northwest. From the initial book idea to its completion, Jo could always find a willing ear, whether in person or over Zoom.

We hope that this volume will provide insights to researchers, practitioners, and policymakers on the importance of listening to and learning from the personal narratives of those engaged every day in working to nudge our education systems—schools, districts, and states—toward greater equity. The book doesn't offer simple solutions or step-by-step instructions because complex problems rooted in persistent, systemic inequities require each individual, whether a first-year principal or a seasoned district administrator—to center their actions on the needs, assets, and values of the communities they serve.

# Introduction

## Jo Smith, University of Auckland, New Zealand

In recent years there have been policy efforts around the globe to create more socially just, equity-minded schools to serve increasingly diverse student populations. In the United States, policy efforts at the state and school district level have focused on recruitment and retention of teachers and school leaders whose ethnic and racial background mirror that of their students. In New Zealand where I now teach, the policy approach at the national level has been to legislate that schools reflect and integrate *te reo Māori* (the indigenous Māori language); *tikanga Māori* ("cultural values and practices"); *mātauranga Māori* (a concept that refers to Māori knowledge); and *te ao Māori* ("Māori worldview") in the schooling system.

One impetus behind state and district policies aimed at cultural responsiveness in the United States is that the diversity of the teacher workforce has not kept pace with increases in student diversity. According to the U.S. Department of Education, in 2020 over half of the nation's K–12 students were children of color while about 80 percent of the educator workforce was White. Numerous studies have highlighted that teachers of color contribute to better academic, behavioral, and socioemotional outcomes for their students.[1] Students with teachers of the same race are less likely to be suspended, more likely to be referred to gifted programs, and more likely to complete high school and go to college.[2] Research has found that having just one Black teacher in grades 3–5 reduces the probability of low-income Black boys dropping out of high school by 39 percent.[3] Moreover, increasing teacher workforce diversity has been shown to benefit all students as diverse teachers bring a varied set of experiences and perspectives beyond those of homogenous teaching populations.[4]

In addition to the benefits associated with a diverse teaching staff, a wide array of empirical research shows that teachers tend to mis-evaluate students of different races on subjective assessments and show a lack of awareness of racial privilege.[5] Teachers' biases affect how they treat different groups of students, potentially perpetuating existing racial achievement gaps. Research has found that 55 percent of teachers in the United States demonstrate a pro-White or anti-Black implicit bias and 15 percent an explicit bias.[6]

Given the range of benefits of a diverse teacher workforce, many school districts and states in the United States have adopted policies aimed at increasing teacher diversity. Some states have implemented policies of home-growing teachers, recruiting potential educators to work in the communities they grew up in to support the diversification of the teacher workforce. However, these policies have been met with persistent barriers such as the costs of state licensure exams and feelings of isolation among minority teaching candidates at predominantly White institutions.[7] The threat of student loan debt also prevents some diverse candidates from enrolling in credentialing programs with the knowledge that the loans will be hard to pay off on a teacher's salary.[8]

In 2020, fifteen states had included teacher diversity policies in their response to federal policy aimed at improving student achievement.[9] Nine states had pledged "to revise, enact or remove state policies that will address specific challenges for both diversifying the educator workforce and ensuring all educators are culturally responsive in practice.[10] For example, a state policy in Connecticut requires the state to hire a minimum of 250 minority teachers state-wide each year;[11] a state policy in New Jersey aims to recruit men of color into the teaching profession;[12] and a state policy in Oregon calls for increasing students' access to educators who more closely mirror the K–12 student population.[13]

Despite these attempts at increasing teacher diversity through legislation, diversity goals remain elusive, some of them representing decades of aspiration with little result. For example, Oregon legislators enacted the Minority Teacher Act in 1991 to increase the diversity of the teacher workforce to better reflect the diversity of the state's student population.[14] These goals remain unmet over 30 years later. As the diversity of Oregon's students has increased over that time period, the vast majority of the teacher workforce has remained White, with 36 percent of students in the state of Oregon identifying as ethnic minorities but only 8 percent of the teaching population.[15] The state's 2016 Educator Equity report found an overall increase in teacher diversity of just slightly over 1 percent, falling far short of legislative goals.[16] It seems that policy alone is insufficient to attain a diverse teacher workforce.

Indeed, a study I was part of in 2018 that looked at efforts to recruit non-White teachers in three states—New York, California, and Colorado—highlighted how a national teacher shortage created a limited pool of applicants, with few teachers of color and few male teachers applying for positions.[17] Study participants reported that aspirational policy and school recruitment efforts were futile when there weren't credentialed candidates available. As one participant reported, "It's not lost on us that it's a national issue that we have so few teachers of color."

Even if they are able to recruit diverse teachers, schools struggle to retain them. As one school leader in the study reflected, "If we only see this as a recruitment issue, we're sort of missing the boat. We went back and looked at the experience of people of color within our organization, and . . . we realized that people of color were leaving us at a rate higher than the general population."

My coeditor Elisabeth Kim writes in chapter 1 about the leaders in the above-mentioned study and the motivations and mechanisms that drove them to work in diverse schools. She finds that many leaders traveled nontraditional pathways to leadership in diverse schools.

The challenges schools in the United States face in recruiting and retaining diverse teachers are not for a lack of trying, and their efforts are supported by state policies, so education leaders are faced with trying to implement socially just, equity-minded reforms with the teachers they have. Chapters 2 and 5 of this book look at some such efforts. In chapter 2, Iton Udosenata details his efforts to move the needle on equity in two Oregon high schools—Cottage Grove High School and North Eugene High School—the setbacks he faced, and his persistence to inspire others to engage in equity-minded work. Chapter 5 showcases Gustavo Balderas's work in Oregon and now the State of Washington to take intentional steps to recruit and retain school and district leaders of color.

In New Zealand, education policy is enacted at the national level and implemented at the school level with oversight by individual school boards. In 2020 the New Zealand government adopted new legislation, *The Education and Training Act 2020*,[18] that focus on meeting the obligations of the Treaty of Waitangi, a treaty enacted in 1840 between the indigenous Māori population and the settler population from Great Britain. The 2020 act is a significant change from earlier legislation: The Education Act of 1989 includes several references to *tikanga Māori* (Māori cultural values and practices). However these were in reference to te reo Māori–medium schools, instruction, and teaching practice. The 2020 act makes it a central concept for the whole schooling system. School boards in all schools in New Zealand are now tasked with oversight by:

- working to ensure that plans, policies, and local curriculum reflect local *tikanga Māori*, *mātauranga Māori*, and *te ao Māori*
- taking all reasonable steps to make instruction available in *te reo Māori* and *tikanga Māori*; and
- achieving equitable outcomes for Māori students.[19]

One effort to meet this policy aspiration has been *Te Ahu o te Reo Māori*, which aims to grow and strengthen schools' ability to integrate te reo Māori in classrooms.[20] This program was piloted in four regions in 2020 with the goal of being more than a te reo Māori language program. It is held up as an opportunity for teachers to engage and understand a te ao Maori worldview and to engage in cultural practices, narratives, and histories relevant to New Zealand and to the system that supports the education of all students.[21] It remains to be seen what the impact of this program will be in increasing equity and social justice in schools across the country. In the meantime, schools in New Zealand and across the globe are faced with meeting the needs of the students they serve today.

In chapter 7, Mona Halcomb discusses policies that the State of Oregon has implemented in order to improve access to educational opportunities for Native American students including changes to the teacher certification process for the Master Teacher in Language License. Oregon's Teacher Standards and Practices Commission worked with the tribes in Oregon to find alternative ways to allow heritage language teachers into the classroom.

In chapter 8, Deborah Lomax writes about the challenges faced by Muslim students in New Zealand's public education system. She describes the paradox that exists between Muslim communities' right to freedom of religious expression, a right at odds with New Zealand's secular national curriculum that reflects the country's bicultural legal status with the indigenous Māori people. Chapter 3 offers lessons learned from a research-practice partnership between the Syracuse City School District, the Jamesville-DeWitt School District, the West-Genesee School District, and Syracuse University in the State of New York to engage together in the practice of equity audits. Chapter 4 describes the virtual reality experiences created by SHIFT founder Wendy Morgan in an effort to increase teachers' empathy and foster a sense of belonging in schools. In Chapter 6, George Theoharis, Sarah Lent, and Kimana Kibriani report on leaders' efforts to create more authentically inclusive services for students with disabilities. Their narratives come from five schools and school districts from the Northeast, the Midwest, and the West Coast spanning elementary through high school.

An overarching theme of this book is to rely on the personal narratives of school and district leaders in explorations of equity work. When we are exposed to the stories of people's lived experiences, we are better able to empathize and create inclusive and welcoming schooling environments for students. Thus many of the chapters in this book bring in the personal narratives of teachers and leaders from a variety of different backgrounds (e.g., Native American, Muslim, Latinx, and African American) to ground their lessons about leadership in their experiences as students, teachers, parents, and even grandparents.

Narrative inquiry is often used in socio-critical studies of the experiences of educators.[22] It involves gathering people's stories and examining the meanings participants ascribe to their experiences in an effort to gain insight into the "complexity of human lives."[23] Narrative inquiry mirrored the sense-making activities described by one of the participants in a study Elizabeth and I were involved with that she reports on in chapter 1: "In one of our early leadership retreats, we did our origin stories and how they inform our work . . . All of us came through these very different stories but the roads . . . lead us to see this as really important work."

We follow a long tradition of narrative research treating participants' stories as a means to understand how they experience the world,[24] their identity,[25] and their role as education leaders[26] and to help us identify their motivations for pursuing leadership.[27] Moreover the descriptiveness of a story "reveals meanings behind actions, meanings that typically go unseen."[28] As Crow et al.[29] point out, narratives can be particularly useful tools in unpacking leadership dispositions and behaviors as people's stories impact how they "come to understand themselves and how they act as embodied beings in the world." In other words, one's stories of self can impact identity formation, and identity can drive behavior.[30]

This volume offers a sense of hope through glimpses into the practices of education leaders in the United States and New Zealand as well as their lived experiences. None of the stories told offers a foolproof formula for achieving the goal of socially just, equity-minded schools. They each present the inherent complexities of enacting change in schools and school systems and the blunders that happen along the way. Each chapter begins by offering key takeaways and ends with reflecting questions to push us all to work toward moving aspiration into action. This volume begins with the premise that equity doesn't just happen and so offers ideas for leaders about how to engage with communities in meaningful and productive ways, how to keep stoking their passion and dedication to face the next hurdle, as well as a reminder to pause and celebrate small successes along the way and always to listen to each other's stories.

## NOTES

1. E.g., Coburn, 2020; Egalite et al., 2014; Grissom et al., 2017; Lindsay & Hart, 2017.
2. Grissom et al., 2017.
3. Gershenson et al. 2017.

4. E.g., Carver-Thomas, 2018; Irizarry, 2007; Mikulyuk & Braddock, 2016.
5. Durand & Tavaras, 2020.
6. Starck et al., 2020.
7. Wallace & Gagen, 2019.
8. Fiddiman, 2020.
9. Ujifusa, 2019.
10. CSSO, 2018.
11. Lyons, 2019.
12. O'Dea, 2019.
13. Chief Education Office, 2019.
14. Smith et al., 2022.
15. Chief Education Office, 2016.
16. Chief Education Office, 2016.
17. Smith et al., 2022.
18. https://www.legislation.govt.nz/act/public/2020/0038/latest/LMS170676.html
19. https://www.legislation.govt.nz/act/public/2020/0038/latest/LMS170676.html
20. See: https://www.education.govt.nz/our-work/overall-strategies-and-policies/te-ahu-o-te-reo-maori-fostering-education-in-te-reo-maori/
21. Ministry of Education, 2020.
22. Clandinin & Connelly, 2000.
23. Josselson, 2006, p. 4.
24. Connelly & Clandinin, 1990.
25. Giddens, 1991.
26. E.g., Crow et al., 2017; Danzig, 1999.
27. Slater, 2011.
28. Danzig, 1999, p.119.
29. Crow et al., 2017, p. 271.
30. Burke & Stets, 2009.

# REFERENCES

Burke, P. J., & Stets, J. E. (2009). *Identity theory*. Oxford University Press.
Carver-Thomas, D. (2018). *Diversifying the Teaching Profession: How to Recruit and Retain Teachers of Color*. Learning Policy Institute.
Chief Education Office. (2019). *2019 Oregon Educator Equity Report*. Chief Education Office.
Chief Education Office. (2016). *2016 Oregon Educator Equity Report*. Chief Education Office.
Clandinin, D. J., & Connelly, F. M. (2000). *Narrative inquiry: Experience and story in qualitative research*. Jossey-Bass.
Coburn, J. (2020). Teacher diversity starts with belonging. *Achieving and Succeeding with Teacher Diversity, 15*(20).

Connelly, F. M., & Clandinin, D. J. (1990). Stories of experience and narrative inquiry. *Educational Researcher, 19*(5), 2–14. https://doi.org/10.3102/0013189X019005002

Council of Chief State School Officers. (2019). *A vision and guidance for a diverse and learner-ready teacher workforce.* https://ccsso.org/resource-library/vision-and-guidance-diverse-and-learner-ready-teacher-workforce

Danzig, A. (1999). How might leadership be taught? The use of story and narrative to teach leadership. *International Journal of Leadership in Education, 2*(2), 117–131. https://doi.org/10.1080/136031299293147

Durand, T. M., & Tavaras, C. L. (2020). Countering complacency with radical reflection: Supporting White teachers in the enactment of critical multicultural praxis. *Education and Urban Society, 53*(2), 146–162. https://doi.org/10.1177/0013124520927680

Egalite, A., Kisida, B., & Winters, M. (2015). Representation in the classroom: The effect of own-race teachers on student achievement. *Economics of Education Review, 45,* 44–52. doi:10.1016/j.econedurev.2015.01.007

Fiddiman, B. (2020). To attract racially diverse teachers, reduce student loan debt. *Achieving and Succeeding with Teacher Diversity, 15*(20).

Gershenson, S., Hart, C., Lindsay, C. and Papageorge, N. W. (2017). The long-run impacts of same-race teachers. IZA Discussion Paper No. 10630. https://ssrn.com/abstract=2940620

Giddens, A. (1991). *Modernity and self-identity.* Stanford University Press.

Grissom, J. A., Rodriguez, L. A., and Kern, E. C. (2017). Teacher and principal diversity and the representation of students of color in gifted programs: Evidence from national data. *The Elementary School Journal, 117*(3), 396–422.

Irizarry, J. G. (2007). "Home-Growing" teachers of color: Lessons learned from a town-grown partnership. *Teacher Education Quarterly, 34*(4), 87–102.

Josselson, R. (2006). Narrative research and the challenge of accumulating knowledge. *Narrative Inquiry, 16*(1), 3–10. https://doi.org/10.1075/ni.16.1.03jos

Lindsay, C. A. and Hart, C. M. D. (2017). Teacher race and school discipline: Are students suspended less often when they have a teacher of the same race? *Education Next, 17*(1), 72–78.

Lyons, K. (2019). Bill requiring more minority teachers in connecticut schools goes to Lamont. *The CT Mirror.* https://ctmirror.org/2019/06/04/bill-requiring-more-minority-teachers-in-connecticut-schools-goes-to-lamont-for-signing/

Mikulyuk, A. B., & Braddock, J. H. (2016). K-12 School diversity and social cohesion: Evidence in support of a compelling state interest. *Education and Urban Society, 50*(1), 5–37. https://doi.org/10.1177/0013124516678045

O'Dea, C. (2019). Lawmakers seeking more diversity among NJ's public school teachers. *NY Spotlight News.* https://www.njspotlightnews.org/2019/02/19-02-07-lawmakers-look-to-increase-diversity-among-njs-public-school-teachers/

Slater, C. L. (2011). Understanding principal leadership: An international perspective and a narrative approach. *Educational Management Administration & Leadership, 39*(2), 219–227. https://doi.org/10.1177/1741143210390061

Smith, J., Porter, L., Harrison, B. J., & Wohlstetter, P. (2022). Barriers to increasing teacher diversity: The need to move beyond aspirational legislation. *Education and Urban Society.* *https://doi.org/10.1177/00131245221076086*

Starck, J. G., Riddle, T., Sinclair, S., & Warikoo, N. (2020). Teachers are people too: Examining the racial bias of teachers compared to other American adults. *Educational Researcher, 49*(4), 273–284. https://doi.org/10.3102%2F0013189X20912758"doi.org/10.3102/0013189X20912758

Ujifusa, A. (2019). Groups tell Washington to make teacher diversity a priority, but how? *Education Week.* https://www.edweek.org/education/

Wallace, D. L., & Gagen, L. M. (2019). African American males' decisions to teach: Barriers, motivations, and supports necessary for completing a teacher preparation program. *Education and Urban Society, 52*(3), 415–432. https://doi.org/10.1177/0013124519846294

*Chapter 1*

# Motivations and Mechanisms

## *Stories of Education Leadership Pathways*

### Elisabeth Crowell Kim, California State University, Monterey Bay

**KEY TAKEAWAYS**

- There is a growing need for equity-minded and social justice–oriented leaders who are better able to retain diverse teachers, more likely to stay in urban schools, better able to contribute to higher achievement of diverse students, and better able to create inclusive environments.
- Education leaders in this study were drawn to diverse schools due to motivations such as cultural responsiveness, critical self-awareness, and a social–justice orientation as well as mechanisms such as experience with segregation and integration, mentorship, and professional networks.
- Many leaders developed these motivations in their childhood, not as a part of their education leadership certification, traveling nontraditional pathways to leadership in diverse schools.

There is a growing shortage of high-quality education leaders in the United States with attrition particularly acute in urban areas[1] and worsened by the COVID–19 pandemic.[2] In addition, there is a significant representation gap between education leaders and the students they serve[3] with a disproportionate number of White males in leadership positions.[4] As the U.S. student population becomes more diverse,[5] chronic Black, indigenous, and people of color (BIPOC) opportunity gaps increase the urgency for more female and BIPOC leaders. There is a need for equity-minded and social justice–oriented leaders who are adept at "creating schools as spaces of inclusivity."[6] Such leaders are better able to retain diverse teachers, more likely to stay in urban schools, better able to contribute to higher levels of achievement of BIPOC students, and better able to create welcoming, inclusive environments in schools.[7] In this chapter, we offer narrative perspectives from a unique sample of social justice–oriented leaders from diverse schools in five urban areas, exploring their leadership pathways, motivations, mechanisms, and hurdles.

## HOW DID WE CONDUCT THIS STUDY?

Our study of leadership pathways is part of a larger mixed-methods research project that examined a wide range of practices and outcomes among intentionally diverse charter schools (IDCS), including student recruitment, teacher professional development, family and community engagement, and academic outcomes. The sample consists of 72 leaders from 27 IDCS campuses across five jurisdictions in the United States (see Figures 1.1 and 1.2). All of the sample schools met two criteria: (1) they had been in operation for at least three years as of 2016–2017, and (2) they were members of the Diverse Charter Schools Coalition, a membership organization created in 2014 for charter schools deemed diverse by design based on a review of the school's mission statement, diversity data, goals, and strategies (e.g., student enrollment preferences and family outreach strategies).[8]

## WHAT DID WE LEARN?

Narratives from our study participants revealed motivations such as cultural responsiveness, critical self-awareness, and a social-justice orientation as well as mechanisms such as experience with segregation or integration, mentorship, and professional networks that shaped their pathways to leadership

| State | Region | Grade Levels | | |
|---|---|---|---|---|
| | | ES | MS | HS |
| | Bay Area | 1 | 1 | 1 |
| CA | LA | 5 | 5 | 2 |
| | San Diego | 0 | 1 | 1 |
| CO | Denver | 0 | 1 | 1 |
| NY | Brooklyn | 3 | 4 | 1 |
| | **Totals** | **9** | **12** | **6** |

Figure 1.1. Study sample.

| Gender (%) (n=72) | | Race/ethnicity (%) (n=63) | | | | | SES (%) (n=67) | | | | 1st gen college (%) (n=72) | |
|---|---|---|---|---|---|---|---|---|---|---|---|---|
| M | F | Bl | Lat | As | Wh | Mlt | WC | MC | UM | U | Y | N |
| 28 | 72 | 14 | 21 | 8 | 44 | 13 | 44 | 34 | 22 | 0 | 12 | 88 |
| (20) | (52) | (9) | (13) | (5) | (28) | (8) | (29) | (29) | (15) | (0) | (9) | (63) |

**Figure 1.2. Study participants.** *Note:* Not all participants provided responses to all of the demographic questions, so the n varies. Mlt: multi-ethnic; WC: working class, MC: middle class; UM: upper middle class; U: upper class.

positions in diverse schools. Below we discuss each motivation and mechanism, including excerpts from the personal narratives of educational leaders. Some of these leaders' stories showed evidence of one clear motivation or mechanism while others touched on more than one.

## Motivations

### Cultural Responsiveness

Leaders in our sample were motivated to work in diverse schools in part because of their own racial and ethnic identity, gender identity, and experiences. For example, a Persian leader at a Brooklyn school shared how her faith and cultural background as well as experiences in her community influenced her work in diverse schools.

> I had grown up being very involved in Baha'i social and economic development projects and working with communities, so that was definitely what my strength was. I think it just naturally fit. Here I am, eight years later doing this.

Learning another language or being exposed to another culture influenced school leaders' perspectives and motivations as well. A leader at a Denver school described himself as a "White, privileged, straight, Caucasian, middle income, Christian male. I check every single box of privilege. Every single one." He spoke of the "richness of diversity" that came from working with an orphanage in Ecuador through his church and how that experience opened him up to other communities in Denver as well.

School leaders were also drawn to diverse schools because of a culturally responsive curriculum or orientation to curriculum that they found to be more effective with a diverse student body. For example, a Black leader from a low-income background at a Denver school spoke of his experience at one of the historically Black colleges and universities (HBCU) that contributed to his pathway to a diverse school and his belief in the importance of a culturally responsive and sustaining education with a social emotional focus particularly for low-income students of color.

> I got six *F*s in one semester. I should have been put out of school but that's not what they did. The dean had a conversation with me and said "You have to get a 3.0 in summer school. Otherwise, you won't be able to return in the Fall." I didn't have an academic issue. It was a social and emotional issue. My mom was sick going through surgery so I self-medicated. A lot of our kids go through that, especially low–SES kids. When our families are struggling, we start having guilt . . . so we drop out of school.

Many of the schools we visited were in the process of adopting culturally responsive, sustaining, and anti-racist practices that were attractive to school leaders. For example, a bi-racial leader at a Brooklyn middle school spoke of her motivation to join a diverse school because she would be able to implement a culturally responsive curriculum. Similarly, a leader at a California school spoke of the experience of conducting an audit of curricular texts and materials in order to ensure that they were representative of their students.

> We still have the old, dead White guys that are in there but our teachers looked at the demographics of the school and the texts that were in each of the classes and just started to find the places where there wasn't a perspective represented from the people that were sitting in their classrooms.

These schools, like many schools in our sample, were in the process of adopting more culturally relevant texts and materials that they saw as being better aligned with their mission of diversity and inclusivity.

## Critical Self-Awareness

Critical self-awareness factored into the narratives, shaping participants' motivation to follow a pathway toward education leadership. Low-income, BIPOC, and first-generation leaders often spoke of their personal experiences with discrimination in school as a driving force. A working-class, Black, first-generation college student noted the motivation stemming from the critical self-awareness that "I wasn't prepared for college. I wanted to understand what I could do to help people like me." Similarly, for a Black middle-class leader who grew up in Phoenix, Arizona, and attended schools that were almost exclusively White, critical consciousness grew from "a number of experiences as being isolated, of peers being intolerant of me, of teachers being unintentionally harmful." In another case, a low-income, mixed-race, female leader at a Los Angeles school described the critical consciousness that led her to seek a leadership role.

> I come from a mixed-race background. I was raised by a single mom. I received free and reduced price lunch as a kid. I grew up in Colorado and my half-brother

grew up in South LA and our experiences going through public schools and what we've had the opportunity to do afterwards have been very, very different.

The self-awareness of how circumstances can hinder outcomes led this leader to seek out a school with a "mission of excellence and diversity" for a diverse student body.

Critical self-awareness emerges from a range of sources and experiences. Some participants spoke of the critical self-awareness that came from working in a diverse school. A White, middle-class, female leader in a Los Angeles school credited her experiences there to teaching her "about the world and relating to people and issues in other people's lives that I just never had stopped and thought about it or had the chance to think about."

For other participants, critical self-awareness grew out of a formative childhood experience. A White female participant identified experiences from high school and college that transformed her consciousness about race and equity in education, noting, "I dated one of two Black students in my high school. That informed a lot of my thinking . . . because [our] parents actually tried to intervene at that time." Her critical self-awareness was further developed in college, where she "noticed a lot of segregation by race . . . One of my roommates was Japanese. I was trying to get her to join everything and she's like, 'No.' My other roommate was Black and she was like, 'No.'" She hadn't considered that a sense of belonging might be lacking for BIPOC students. "Those experiences I think were helpful for me to think about race in the educational context," she noted, reflecting on her growing critical self-consciousness.

In another case of formative childhood experiences, an Asian leader from a New York school who grew up in a middle-class family reported developing critical self-awareness through accompanying her father who worked with indigenous populations in Asia to develop sustainable crop systems. She noted, "A lot of my schooling was both formal and informal since I would go out with my father into the rice fields and meet with farmers, and learn about how to feed people." Her critical self-awareness led her to join Teach for America (TFA) in search of a more diverse setting after teaching high school in Missouri for five years. She noted that working in diverse schools "makes perfect sense . . . in our public education system if we want to realize *Brown versus Board [of Education]*." Finally, a Persian-American participant reported her critical self-awareness came from childhood experiences of isolation at school.

> I'm a child of two immigrants who came to the States from Iran to study and ended up staying here because they couldn't go back, because the revolution broke out in Iran. I went to public school where I very, very much felt like I

didn't belong . . . If you weren't White and Christian in the school that I was in, you really didn't belong. Everything from my hair, everything about me I think just made me feel left out. I struggled a lot with being proud of who I am as a person and honoring that and being accepted in school.

## Social Justice Orientation

Education leaders were drawn to diverse schools by a passion for social justice, a commitment to educating low-income BIPOC students, and the organizations' diversity missions. For example, a Black education leader at a school in Brooklyn who had once worked in a No Excuses–style charter network explained that she was motivated to be a leader in a school "that didn't treat Black and Brown children like the only way to teach them is like in a prison. I wanted to see . . . how do people view education differently once you involve White children? And it is very different." Similarly, a leader from a Brooklyn school who described herself as "put in the model minority box because my parents are immigrants from West Africa" and who went to a prestigious private school said she was motivated by a social justice orientation: "Kids who are underserved, deserve the kind of education that I received so my goal is just to spread all of that to the masses."

Further, a leader from a school in Los Angeles spoke about the differences in working at another nearby school in which there was some racial but very little socioeconomic diversity which caused her to leave and find a school with a mission and student body that was more aligned with her sense of social justice.

> Our level of diversity is different than what I experienced on the West Side. Even though [they] could sort of meet some of the requirements, it did not feel like I was serving the population that I'm most passionate about whereas here, it's completely different. It actually feels very diverse in terms of socioeconomics, culture, language, privilege, access, political opinions. A lot of times, when the word diversity is used, [people] are just looking for 20 or 30% African-American but the actual experience of diversity isn't there.

Social justice orientations arise from a variety of sources; some participants, for example, were motivated by their experiences in stratified environments and sought to disrupt patterns of inequity. As a leader in a Denver school reported, her experience in a somewhat homogeneous college environment influenced her to work in the field as a form of social justice, noting that college "was a huge shock because it's a low population of students of color who go to college and therefore, graduate from it." She translated this realization into action, working to break cycles of privilege through intentional student recruitment to reach diverse students.

Social justice orientations sometimes were directed at inequities for teachers as well as providing opportunities for diverse students. One mixed-race, low-income, female leader in a Denver school spoke of her experiences as a student and the daughter of a teacher in a rural school and how that influenced her to work in a diverse school as a social justice–oriented leader, noting the motivation of "seeing the way public schools have traditionally treated their educators. And so I was very drawn to [the school] and how they value their educators and how they push for value and how they push students to value education."

Similarly, a leader of a school in Brooklyn described the social-justice motivation that drew him to his leadership path. Having worked at the prestigious Sidwell Friends and SEED charter school in Washington, DC, this multiracial son of a Japanese immigrant strove to create an integrated school to help bridge the home-school divide for students. He described a student at Sidwell Friends from a low-income background for whom coming to school "was space travel every day for her. She would get up on one planet, get on her spaceship, and land on a different planet."

Another leader from a Brooklyn school noted the social justice–oriented motivation of the work, saying, "It's about opportunity. Like when I see . . . my brothers, and sisters, my nephews and nieces that are gonna be fighting for opportunity, it really inspires me to come in and kick ass at work. Like, how can I open up more opportunities?" This Black leader from a low-income background described the realization of how unequal urban schools can be as a motivation to work in a diverse school.

> My niece graduated from a terrible high school in DC. She was ranked second in her class and I [asked her], 'What's your percentile?' . . . Second in her class but in all topics, the highest percentile was 18. In one of them she was like 10 or 11. When I see that in my communities, it's so frustrating that it makes me get up—and want to work even harder.

## Mechanisms

### Experience with Segregated or Integrated Schools as Students or Teachers

Leaders of color who attended segregated schools spoke of the limited opportunities in their schools and how that became a mechanism for working in a different environment. For example, a Black, low-income, female leader in a Brooklyn charter revealed, "I'm a first generation college student and I didn't have the best education. I wasn't prepared for college. I wanted to understand what I could do to help people like me." Similarly, a low-income Latinx male at a Los Angeles school spoke of his experience in college when he first noted the differences in education standards in different parts of the country and how that motivated him to work at a diverse school.

> I graduated in the top 10 percent of my class, 3.7 GPA and my roommate who came from a suburb of Chicago and was middle class graduated with a 2 point something from his high school. I remember talking about our classes in college and being like, "What the hell? How is it possible that I was here?" That was my first glimpse into public education and how we can divide among racial lines because of zip codes. That was pretty hard to accept, to be like, "That's not fair. How do you expect me to compete if I didn't get the same opportunity?"

Leaders also experienced segregation as students through tracking and noticing that BIPOC students were often left out of the highest performing classes, or as this White, working-class, female leader in a San Diego school described, in separate facilities.

> I grew up in a pretty small town and went to a comprehensive high school which was definitely not integrated. We had a pretty high population of migrant workers and so many of the Latino students that went to our school I never saw but were literally in trailers outside the main building.

Similarly, a half-Asian female leader in a Los Angeles school who grew up in the American South spoke of her experience with segregation within supposedly integrated schools.

> Our public schools were technically integrated. It was in the height of busing but looking back, the school was extremely segregated in terms of the way that classes were composed and the way tracks were managed. It felt like multiple schools operating within a school depending what track you were assigned to. I think that being racially ambiguous in a city that was very divided between White and Black shaped a lot of the way I think about education.

Conversely, some White and middle- or upper-middle-income leaders developed a critical consciousness about segregation later in life. As this Denver education leader described it, "I had a very strong K–12 educational experience but it was really not until college that I actually had any awareness of the lack of diversity in my own upbringing." A White Brooklyn school leader experienced segregation as a principal at a traditional public school in New York City in which 100% of the students were Black or Brown and living in poverty and went through a "very contentious turnaround effort." She lived near a school that she described as "one of the more segregated schools in New York City because it screens for performance and behavior. It's 70%

White." Seeing the disparities in the education system led her to turn to work in integrated schools. Another White leader in a school in Brooklyn described her experience with the negative effects of segregation at another school and how she began to develop a critical consciousness leading her to leadership in a more diverse school: "I had experienced such high levels of segregation in the educational sphere . . . I just had a lot of thoughts about why and how and what was happening in those spaces . . . That disconnect was a big driving force for me."

In contrast, some narratives disclosed experiences attending integrated schools and a motivation to continue working in a similar environment, such as this White, middle-income, female leader in a Brooklyn school.

> My parents moved to our town because the public school was so strong. It was one of the first racially integrated school systems in the country. And that was always a big part of my upbringing. That's my reference point for how you learn so much more than just academics. That was my foundation.

A White, middle-income, female school leader at an independent school in Los Angeles spoke of the contrast between her K–12 experience in an integrated school district and her experience in a mostly White college and wanting to recreate her K–12 experience in her professional life.

> In our community, there was something called White flight. We didn't flee. We all just went to school and went through [the public schools] all of my life. They were very integrated. It wasn't until I got to university. I went to a private Catholic school where I was literally in culture shock because it was the first time I was surrounded by nothing but White people. That's not what I grew up in. That really shaped my values of being in a diverse setting and realizing that that was a unique situation . . . My connection to [the school] is really through my childhood experience and the opportunity in [my hometown] to ensure that we are serving a diverse population in all senses of the word.

## *Mentorship and Recruitment*

Some leaders were directly recruited by diverse schools while others, particularly those from underrepresented backgrounds, cited the importance of mentors along their pathway to culturally responsive leadership as described by a low-income Latinx male leader: "My mentor was very intentional about changing your world. He would give you opportunities that you couldn't even begin to imagine. As a first-generation college student, I was a sponge." Mentors encouraged leaders to seek environments more reflective of their values and encouraged them to see their potential as education leaders, such as in the case of a working-class Persian-American who cited the importance of her mentor encouraging her to apply to Teachers College in propelling her down her leadership pathway.

Similarly, a Latinx school leader at a Los Angeles school spoke of his mentor's plan for him which led him to leadership. He reported that after two years of working in the college counselor's office, he told his mentor, the college counselor, that "I wanted her job when she retired—she was near retirement—and she convinced me to start teaching first before I became a counselor. I think she had a plan for me. Anyway, it worked." Mentors offered advice that led our study participants to choose education leadership over other career options. A half-Asian leader at a school in Los Angeles planned to go to law school until her mentor encouraged her to stay in education. She eventually became a school leader, prompted by her mentor's advice. "I didn't really go searching for opportunities but my principal told me, 'I think you'd be great working with other teachers. I want you to interview for it.' I was like, 'I don't know.' I wasn't really thinking about that."

Sometimes mentors played a role in shaping participants' leadership pathways by making them aware of schools they felt would be a good match for their interests and passion. A White, middle-income leader at a Los Angeles school spoke of her mentor's role in making her aware of an opportunity to be the founding principal at the school, noting, "I heard about it from my mentor who happens to be on our board. She had put it in my ear and I kind of ignored it for a while. Then she put it back in my ear." In another case, a working-class Latinx participant noted a mentor suggested applying for a position at a California school because the mentor thought it would be a good fit. Mentors' persistence often made the difference between an idea and a pathway.

*Professional Networks*

Leaders utilized their networks at other charters through graduate school and TFA during their leadership pathways as well. Some schools intentionally recruited underrepresented groups for leadership positions, suggesting a commitment to a culturally responsive and inclusive school environment. For example, as this low-income Black male leader at a Denver school stated, "Almost half the [leadership] team are people of color, women, from all parts of the country. [We] purposely sought out and found people who would fit the vision." Similarly, an Asian leader at a Los Angeles school shared, "I am a woman of color. It's important that my leadership reflects the kids and it's important that the kids see themselves in all of my staff members." A male Latinx leader at a California school agreed, stating,

> Part of it is also looking beyond the numeric diversity of who we enroll. You can't have the diversity of thought and approach and contributions to a classroom, or a community as an institution, without the numbers. So, yes, others can be educated and share that knowledge, but until you have those lived experiences from our students, from our staff, and in our faculty, the diversity doesn't just magically appear.

Many school leaders also did TFA, and that experience became a mechanism for them to eventually lead a diverse school. For example, a half-Asian female leader in Los Angeles spoke of her time in law school in the American South and how it led her to join TFA and eventually start a group of schools as a way to address some of the inequities she witnessed.

> I assumed that since I went to public school that other kids were going to public schools that looked like mine but when I got into these alternative school settings specifically for court-involved youth, I saw the disparity between what I was given in part because of my zip code and what others were receiving.

A middle-class White school leader originally from the Midwest who is now in a Denver school spoke of her experience in college in a Northeastern city and how it contributed to her passion for social justice and her pathway to leadership in a diverse school.

> Moving from Sioux City, Iowa, to Philadelphia was definitely my first exposure to the opportunity gap. I love sports so I got involved in a coaching and middle-school program in West Philadelphia. Part of that program was tutoring. I think that was a shocking experience for me, working with middle school students who were amazing and loved learning but were very, very far behind. I think that experience inspired me to apply to TFA.

## WHAT DO LESSONS LEARNED MEAN FOR EDUCATIONAL LEADERSHIP?

This research reveals a number of lessons learned for school systems and leadership training programs. First, there is a benefit to supporting flexibility of different pathways to leadership that are informed by the local context and the needs of the community. Recruitment practices and leadership training program prerequisites may overlook nontraditional leaders, particularly female leaders of color who are often left out of traditional leadership pathways. Second, an explicit, culturally responsive, social justice component would be beneficial to leadership or administrative credentialing programs. An orientation that includes cultural responsiveness, critical self-awareness, and social justice could motivate and attract a broader array of leadership candidates and help retain them in leadership positions once they arrive at increasingly diverse schools. None of the leaders in our sample spoke of developing such an orientation to leadership during their leadership training programs. It either happened through personal experiences in childhood or college or professional experiences as teachers or even once they had arrived at their school. It is important that leadership and administrative credentialing programs be able to cultivate and further the orientations that many leaders already have within them during their pathway to leadership.

Third, it is important to consider how school systems can leverage the networks built in graduate school and through programs like TFA in order to ensure that nontraditional leaders are able to use them effectively during their job search. Too often female leaders of color are discouraged by a perceived lack of mentors and networks and do not pursue leadership positions. The mentors and networks that they do have access to are not always valued by the traditional leadership pathway process. However, networks can be critically important in helping leaders identify the values that are meaningful to them and finding positions aligned with those values.

Lastly, some schools in our study had their own credentialing programs that were tightly aligned with their mission and values of diversity and inclusivity, which may be attractive to nontraditional leaders. Others had the freedom to recruit leaders through nontraditional means such as using HBCUs and other like-minded schools. Many also spoke of identifying people with promise within their schools and providing them with on-the-job training so that they could one day become leaders. Leaders like these would have been missed through a traditional pathway. Thus it is important that school systems and leadership and credentialing programs begin to consider how they might build more flexibility into their recruitment practices so that they do not overlook nontraditional education leaders.

## REFLECTIVE QUESTIONS

- What is the demographic makeup of the education leaders in your area? How does it match with the demographic backgrounds of the students they serve?
- How can we best recruit nontraditional candidates for education leadership positions?
- What should be taught in education leadership certification programs in order to best prepare future leaders to work in diverse schools?
- How can we use personal narratives in our work to better understand the motivations of education leaders?

## NOTES

1. Bailes & Guthery, 2020.
2. National Association of Secondary School Principals, 2020
3. Grissom et al., 2021.
4. Gates et al., 2004; Ringel et al., 2004; Brown & White, 2010; Crawford & Fuller, 2017; Fuller et al., 2007.
5. de Brey et al., 2019.
6. Khalifa, 2010, 2013; cited in Khalifa et al. 2016, p. 8.
7. Bailes & Guthery, 2020; Grissom & Keiser, 2011; Miller, 2013; Myung et al., 2011.
8. For further details about our study's sample and qualitative and quantitative data collection and analysis, see Wohlstetter et al., 2021.

## REFERENCES

Bailes, L. P., & Guthery, S. (2020). Held down and held back: Systematically delayed principal promotions by race and gender. *AERA Open, 6*(2). https://doi.org/10.1177/2332858420929298

Crawford, E. R., & Fuller, E. J. (2017). A dream attained or deferred? Examination of production and placement of Latino administrators. *Urban Education, 52*(10), 1167–1203. https://doi.org/10.1177/0042085915602537

de Brey, C., Musu, L., McFarland, J., Wilkinson-Flicker, S., Diliberti, M., Zhang, A., Branstetter, C., & Wang, X. (2019). Status and trends in the education of racial and ethnic groups 2018 (NCES 2019–038). National Center for Education Statistics. https://nces.ed.gov/pubs2019/2019038.pdf

Fuller, E., Young, M. D., & Orr, M. T. (2007). Career pathways of principals in Texas. Paper presented at the annual meeting of the American Educational Research Association (AERA).

Gates, S. M., Hamilton, L. S., Martorell, P., Burkhauser, S., Heaton, P., Pierson, A., Baird, M., Vuollo, M., Li, J. J., Lavery, D. C., Harvey, M., & Gu, K. (2004). *Preparing principals to raise student achievement implementation and effects of the New Leaders Program in Ten Districts.* RAND Corporation.

Grissom, J. A., & Keiser, L. R. (2011). A supervisor like me: Race, representation, and the satisfaction and turnover decisions of public sector employees. *Journal of Policy Analysis and Management, 30*(3), 557–580. https://doi.org/10.1002/pam.20579

Grissom, J. A., Egalite, A. J., & Lindsay, C. A. (2021). *How principals affect students and schools: A systematic synthesis of two decades of research.* Wallace Foundation.

Khalifa, M. (2010). Validating social and cultural capital of hyperghettoized at-risk students. *Education and Urban Society, 42*, 620–646. doi:10.1177/0013124510366225

Khalifa, M. A., Gooden, M. A., & Davis, J. E. (2016). Culturally responsive education leadership: A synthesis of the literature. *Review of Educational Research.* https://doi.org/10.3102/0034654316630383

Miller, A. (2013). Principal turnover and student achievement. *Economics of Education Review, 36,* 60–72. https://doi.org/10.1016/j.econedurev.2013.05.004

Myung, J., Loeb, S., & Horng, E. (2011). Tapping the principal pipeline: Identifying talent for future school leadership in the absence of formal succession management programs. *Educational Administration Quarterly, 47*(5), 695–727. https://doi.org/10.1177/0013161x11406112

National Association of Secondary School Principals [NASSP]. (2020). *Principals say pandemic conditions are accelerating their plans to leave the principalship.* https://www.nassp.org/2020/08/21/principals-say-pandemic-conditions-are-accelerating-their-plans-to-leave-the-principalship/

Ringel, J., Gates, S., Chung, C., Brown, A., & Ghosh-Dastidar, B. (2004). *Career paths of school administrators in Illinois: Insights from an analysis of state data.* RAND Corporation.

Wohlstetter, P., Cordes, S., Smith, J., & Kim, E. (2021). *Moving the needle on desegregation: Performance outcomes and implementation lessons from Diverse-by-Design charter schools.* https://www.tc.columbia.edu/media/news/images/2021/august/TC-Diverse-by-Design_Final.pdf

*Chapter 2*

# Enacting Culturally Responsive School Leadership

## *Experiences Working Toward Institutional Change*

Iton Udosenata, Salem-Keizer
Public Schools, Oregon

### KEY TAKEAWAYS

- Don't wait for buy in. Leading for equity is too important to wait for the hesitant to provide a green light before moving forward.
- Embrace boldness. You have to take chances when hiring in order to disrupt the status quo.
- It isn't enough to change systems within a school; community voice and embedding community and culture in day-to-day events is crucial.
- Framing matters. Design a school environment that serves as an extension of students' culture and community.
- Believe in the process. Steadfast and unwavering leadership inspires others to take chances.
- Celebrate the victories and learn from the flops.

Our journey as culturally responsive leaders is often driven by our eagerness to learn from the experiences of others who blazed a trail in the field or unlocked a breakthrough strategy that led to more-equitable schools and outcomes. We commonly engage in our learning as leaders for equity through masterful presentations at conferences and prose from renowned authors who specialize in equity. The content of equity-centered professional development is anchored in the success stories of schools; after all it is the successes that inspire leaders to innovate and act within their own respective practice. Yet there is much to be learned from attempts that fell flat, didn't quite meet the mark, or outright backfired. I served as a high school principal of two schools over the course of seven years. The first, Cottage Grove High School (CGHS), was situated in a small de-industrialized lumber town in Oregon with high levels of generational poverty; the other school, North Eugene High School (NEHS), was located in an urban setting, also with high levels of poverty, and was the most ethnically and socioeconomically diverse school within the Eugene school district. Both schools had their unique set of circumstances that called for culturally responsive strategies to meet students' needs.

During my tenure as principal at these two schools, I coordinated several efforts to foster equitable outcomes and welcoming learning environments for all students, especially those who had historically been discriminated against, disenfranchised, or dismissed for reasons beyond their control. I'm proud of the accomplishments that occurred in my time as principal of CGHS and NEHS. Both schools experienced measurably improved academic outcomes with the CGHS graduation rate rising to 96% by the time I departed, the fourth-highest graduation rate in the state of Oregon at the time. NEHS had the lowest graduation rate in the district when I arrived in the fall of 2017; at 70% this was two percent below the state average. The NEHS graduation rate increased by 11% in my first year and grew to 86% after my second year as principal. Importantly, we were able to change the narrative at both schools and rethink what it meant to remove barriers and create opportunities for students. There were numerous equity initiatives that undoubtedly worked for kids, like when we repurposed Associated Student Body funds so that students did not have to pay to participate in athletics, or when we performed an equity scan to build a case for making Advanced Placement classes more accessible for our heritage Spanish speakers and students of color. These efforts took teamwork, creative thinking, and an intense focus on what it meant to lead for equity. Naturally we gravitate toward sharing the moments that define our achievements; however, I had my fair share of initiatives that were well-intentioned but didn't move the dial when it came to equitable outcomes. I made botched hires, errant leadership moves, and ate crow more times than I care to admit. But this is part of the journey, and these experiences I often underscore when speaking with aspiring administrators and colleagues during planning sessions. Though they are unconventional anecdotes for discussions like these, I believe there are a lot of lessons to be learned from the disappointment of not getting it right. While it is not the prevailing narrative, our shortcomings should not be processed as something to be ashamed of; rather, these setbacks should challenge us in ways that make us better as leaders for equity and should share the stage with our feel-good equity work rather than be tucked away in our memory banks never to be accessed again. In this chapter I will access these memories to offer the lessons learned from bold equity moves that sometimes worked out and sometimes did not. As you read, contemplate how my experiences connect to your own and how our efforts, for better or worse, can inspire and effect change.

## DON'T WAIT FOR BUY IN

One of the greatest mistakes I've made as an equity leader was feeling like I needed to generate a certain level of buy in before taking bold moves to implement an equity driven initiative. This was the case in 2016 when I laid the groundwork for implementing the AVID program (see www.avid.org) at CGHS. After a year of information gathering, lobbying the central office for support, and multiple discussions with the school leadership team, I decided against moving forward with onboarding AVID. I made this decision even after 85% of staff communicated, in a survey, that they were in favor of bringing the program to our school. The reason I decided to postpone this initiative was because I believed it was too important to fail and I didn't think AVID would thrive without the support of critical stakeholders; so I chose not to proceed with the initiative. This was a decision that I still regret partly because of the opportunity that students missed out on but more so because I knew, internally, it was what was right for kids. While it is important to always be measured, we should not compromise when it comes to the well-being of students. Over the years I have deconstructed why leaders rely so heavily on buy in and why it is a mistake to wait for consensus to take action.

Most of the time leaders seek buy in because of a lack of confidence or the fear that other influential stakeholders will collude to box them in, leaving their initiative to languish in endless leadership discussions before being abandoned when the next initiative cycle rolls through. Some leaders use this consensus process as a cover that will shield their leadership if things go sideways. If a principal were to take action on an initiative, like instituting AVID for instance, and the staff did not commit to investing in the program, the administrator would run the risk of being viewed as a top-down leader, as an authoritarian who isn't willing to collaborate. Suddenly that principal would feel intense pressure for the initiative to succeed while knowing there are many reluctant staff members. This is a risky endeavor and it can be damaging to a principal's reputation or career, so it is understandable why a leader would rely on buy in before proceeding with significant changes that will impact the system or school climate.

Leading for equity is too important to wait for the collective to provide a green light before moving forward, however. Further, there are many worthy initiatives that will not see the light of day if leaders wait for buy in. Teachers want to be part of the decision making process and will go to great lengths to ensure opinions and ideas are taken into consideration in any planning process. There is no doubt that teacher input is important. Teachers also want to be given explicit direction on vision, mission, and process. I have found that people actually want to be told what to do, and the only condition is that leaders are acting with transparency. Dr. Gustavo Balderas (see chapter 5) is one of the best at this and someone that I learned from when it came to making important decisions with resolve and not waiting for buy in. Teacher voice and process need to be balanced. Too many voices leads to saturation, and the old adage of having too many cooks in the kitchen means diminishing returns, which prevents the work from being done.

There was a trade-off to this decision to not implement AVID. While the graduation rate at CGHS was above 90%, many potential first-generation college students missed out on a program that had been proven to help this very population develop the skills and know-how to get into college.

## THE IMPORTANCE OF COMMUNITY VOICE

Culturally responsive leadership has emerged as an essential component in equity work over the years. As a culturally responsive leader, I learned that it isn't enough to change systems within a school to build equity and inclusion in schools; nor is it enough to stay current on matters related to equity and inclusion if the community is not at the heart of this work. An intense focus on community helps to build bridges between school and community, strengthen ownership for all groups, and foster long-term goodwill.

It is important to integrate community and local culture into decision making, otherwise school may feel like it is "being done" to our diverse learners from outsiders instead of being carried out in partnership with our community and families. This was especially important in 2019 when the state of Oregon passed House Bill 3427, the Student Success Act (SSA). The SSA included the Student Investment Account (SIA) that required community engagement, especially with "focal" students and families: students who are members of tribes, students of color, students with disabilities, emergent bilingual students, and students navigating poverty, houselessness, and foster care. The SIA was intended to close the achievement gap for historically underserved groups by focusing on academics and social emotional supports. To receive SIA funds, schools needed to solicit feedback from their school community about student needs and the most important aspects of education. This was fulfilled through extensive listening sessions at schools, faith-based centers, and local community centers. These listening sessions were also performed in a variety of languages. SIA also required an SIA committee that was composed of ethnically diverse community leaders. Along with extensive listening sessions, we conducted surveys for students, staff, and families to understand what students needed to feel connected to school and to have a sense of belonging. I'm not sure how long it would have taken us to find this out without the input from community leaders.

Through this process we learned of the high value our community placed on mental health, each student's sense of belonging, and a culturally relevant curriculum and that these were among the most important elements of school. At Salem Keizer Public Schools we used community input to repurpose our investments in social emotional learning and mental health supports. This resulted in an investment in 15 counselors, 11 social workers, and community outreach specialists. At NEHS, we encouraged students to get involved in extracurricular activities by waiving athletic fees to remove barriers. These investments and initiatives were essential to the success and well-being of our diverse learners and resulted in positive outcomes and increased attendance and achievement for our respective groups. I am doubtful if the implementation of these investments would have been as effective without the input of community voice.

## EMBEDDING COMMUNITY AND CULTURE IN DAY-TO-DAY EVENTS

Not every school district has the resources that SIA made available for community investments, and that is okay. There are many creative ways to generate community involvement that don't cost a dime. At NEHS we worked closely with our Indian Education Program and Native American community leaders to elevate the presence of Native American culture in our day-to-day school operations, school curriculum, and school events. Every other Friday we welcomed Native American Education Director Joe Brainard to campus where he would sell fry-bread in the school commons during lunch with proceeds going to the NEHS Native American Club. We worked closely with Mr. Brainard and our Native American Club to develop a day-long celebration for Indigenous Peoples Day. This event, intentionally, was scheduled the day before the Thanksgiving holiday to honor Native American heritage and featured a modern pow-wow dance, a Native American student panel, and educational talks by native elders about the history of Native American boarding schools in America.

Though NEHS had the most ethnically diverse population in the district, Black students and students with African heritage represented only 2% of the student population (N = 30). With such a small level of representation, the experience of Black students was one of isolation that led to a yearning for community and representation. To support our Black student population we knew we needed adult advocates who had a shared cultural background and understood the experiences of Black students in a school with a small Black population. At NEHS, we relied heavily on Ann Christianson, an African-American community member, longtime NEHS staff member, and parent of two Black NEHS graduates. Students referred to Ms. Christianson as "Momma"; she was the staff liaison for the Black Student Union; and her room was open all day for students to get support, advocacy, and a place to congregate. Ms. Christianson was very connected to our greater Black community within the Eugene Metro area. Christianson routinely leveraged her community resources to elevate inclusion and cultural presence for Black students. She did this by coordinating volunteers who could provide mentorship for students, organizing African-American family nights to engage families as well as organizing college student–aid events to teach families how to access college. One of the most impactful events on campus was the Martin Luther King Jr. assembly that took place each January. This event was organized by the NEHS Black Student Union under the guidance of Ms. Christianson. The program included speeches by prominent Black leaders from the community and local universities. The days leading up to the event, the entire student body learned the history of "Lift Every Voice and Sing" along with the lyrics. The pre-teaching primed our students for the singing of "Lift Every Voice" at the assembly, led by Andiel Brown and the University of Oregon Gospel Choir. During the singing of "Lift Every Voice" 1,000 students of all races and ethnicity along with community members stood in unity and swayed in the bleachers of the NEHS gymnasium and sang in unison. This is the power of community and education.

One of my favorite programs that connected the community with the school was the Clear Thinking Pipeline. This event was originally pitched to me as the School-to-Prison Pipeline Forum by longtime African-American community leader, coach, and equity leader Leon Lincoln. The idea was to provide a space for students to think deeper about how the choices they make now either expand opportunities or lead to detrimental consequences. It was also intended to get students to understand how institutions work, especially those of higher education, so that they could enter those spaces with a better understanding of how to be successful. The event took place in two segments. First, a variety of local African-American and Latinx panelists from the academic sector, business sector, correctional industry, and human services (health and law, mental health) shared their experiences in a dialogue facilitated by an emcee. Then students attended breakout sessions of their choice for deeper conversations with the panelists of their choice. Afterward students reflected during their social studies class to determine how their experiences at the Clear Thinking Pipeline would inform their long- and short-term academic and personal goals.

I see events like the Clear Thinking Pipeline as a lynch-pin between community and academics. It allows students to see people who share their cultural experiences and helps students make sense of the importance of their own academic journey. It's a fusion between the oft disconnected presence of academic supports and cultural liaisons that should both serve to enhance student experiences and opportunity.

## BELIEVE IN THE PROCESS

We live in an outcome-driven society that places a high value on the final product. This is depicted in mainstream media through home make-over programs, and in social media through physical transformation videos that show the stark contrast of before and after images. Rarely do we see the metamorphosis that transpires between points A and Z of these processes. This focus on *before* and *after* plays out in the world of public education as well, but the struggle that occurs in the journey is routinely omitted, making it difficult for staff to accept the ups and downs of a journey that always plays out as an innocent rise in the consciousness of the mainstream and in testimonials at educational conferences.

One of the most trying yet rewarding processes I led as a principal was a visioning process at NEHS between 2017 and 2020. There was consensus among the staff and community that NEHS needed a make-over to help the school community re-establish its identity within the greater Eugene area. For many years NEHS had a reputation as a school that was rough around the edges in every sense of the phrase and had never bounced back after the dissolution of a small schools model in the 2010s. It was a reputation that stigmatized students and caused socially mobile parents in the school feeder area to send their children elsewhere. As a result, the school population plummeted from 1,200 students in 2010 to 800 students in 2017. In my first year, the district contracted with regional consultants to help with visioning with an emphasis on branding and identity. Our first iteration of the visioning process flopped.

In the fall of 2018 we hit reset and attempted the visioning process again. The 2017 campaign had focused on developing a visioning process with all of the elementary and middle schools in the secondary feeder area. The second go-around of the process focused solely on NEHS and no other schools.

The 2018 visioning process was led by the same consultation group, and the activities included several listening sessions with staff, community, parents, and students. The student listening sessions were intensive and took a few weeks to complete. This process culminated in a big reveal of the final product, which included graphics and maxims that could be used for branding and long-term planning.

I'd had a year to learn the sensibilities of my staff and knew that they often focused on the negative when they were together in a group. Before the reveal I attempted to get ahead of any potential skepticism by scripting out whom we would call on for comments in advance with my administrative team. I described this plan as a pre-determined script similar to those that professional wrestlers hash out prior to taking the ring. Our strategy was to call on the most sensible staff members and ride the momentum of their comments to drive the conversation and feedback we provide the consultants. But when the meeting began our assistant principal deviated from this plan and called on a veteran staff member with a reputation for being unmercifully critical of just about everything that was put before the staff.

Before we knew it, the staff was making one negative comment after another about the maxims and graphics related to our visioning recommendations. They were brutal, discrediting everything from word choice to the color scheme of the visioning recommendations. The discussion reached a point when I had no choice but to interrupt the conversation. I stepped into the center of the library where we were seated and got everyone's attention by putting my fist in the air in the same manner that a teacher does when getting a class's attention. I then launched into an extemporaneous story about Joel Embiid, a professional basketball player for the Philadelphia 76ers, with the nickname "the Process." I discussed Embiid's career arc and went into detail about how he entered the NBA with high expectations but had many setbacks early in his career that limited his impact. Whenever Embiid was asked about his struggles to stay healthy and live up to the expectations, he would consistently respond by stating, "I need to trust the process." I continued by sharing that Embiid went on to become an NBA All-Star and helped lead his team to the playoffs and become championship contenders. But he didn't do this without struggle, and our staff, like Embiid needed to trust the process. This talk was enough to redirect the negative energy in the room and send a message to the staff that we needed to lean into the visioning process.

The following year we began a third iteration of the visioning process. In my talk with the staff, I shared that visioning isn't something that someone does to you. I continued by sharing that none of our initiatives were going to be fruitful unless we stopped waiting for someone to do something to us and began changing our own disposition as a staff. This begins with trusting in a process and leaning into the process even when it is bumpy or seems futile.

To this day I don't know that the visioning process was ever successful and would argue that it would not meet the standards of any before-and-after transformation. However, NEHS underwent a significant transformation in that time. Socially mobile families weren't fleeing to other schools at the same rate, school achievement soared, and NEHS began to shift its reputation from rough around the edges to that of "a school where there is something for every student." The transformation was not easy. There were a lot of difficult conversations, botched visioning processes, and mishaps along the way. But through it all the staff leaned into the struggle even when our efforts seemed misdirected. As leaders we need to be unflinching in our own belief in the process in order to inspire others to take chances, celebrate the victories, and learn from the flops.

## FINAL THOUGHTS

As administrators, we come into positions where we're intimidated for one reason or another. Maybe we think we're out of our class. Maybe we think the job is too big. Whatever the case is, there is a tendency for an administrator or a leader to put too much pressure on themselves, and in doing that we don't allow, in boxing terms, our "hands to go." We don't allow space for creativity, space for taking chances, space for imagining what can be. I hope that readers will learn from my journey and experiences that it's okay to take chances and it's okay to fail from time to time because that's the only way that we're really going to make changes. While playing it safe feels good because it gives us a sense of security, it rarely creates or fosters real change and especially in the communities that need change the most.

Sometimes we get so enthralled with the idea of elevating equity by diversifying our workforce that we rush into hiring applicants who are mismatched for our school but fit our desired applicant profile. Looking back, I don't regret any hiring decisions even if they didn't work out in the end. You have to be willing to take chances to disrupt the status quo. Too often hiring administrators balk at hiring a candidate with tremendous potential because the candidate doesn't have enough experience or doesn't seem ready.

Reframing school design so that community and equity are at the center of decisions honors students and the culture they bring to school. This is a shift from dated practices that demand that students conform to established school culture and norms. In Salem and NEHS, the priority was to design a school environment that acted as an extension of students' culture and community. By soliciting the community for student needs, working with community partners, and prioritizing cultural inclusion, we created a pathway for deeper engagement for all students, enhanced their experiences, and elevated outcomes for all students.

## REFLECTIVE QUESTIONS

1. What lessons have you learned from a failed attempt to effect change and how will they inform your work?
2. Who or what are the connectors in your school and greater school community?
3. What is a bold move you can make now without waiting for buy in?
4. Outcomes aside, what is the most important equity process to be tackled? How will you inspire others to believe in this process?
5. How will you leverage your sphere of influence in your school community?

*Chapter 3*

# Culturally Sustaining and Socially Just Leadership Practice
## *Engaging* in *Collaborative Equity Audits*

George Theoharis, Syracuse University; Christine A. Ashby, Syracuse University; Sarah Gentile, West Genesee Central School District; Nate Franz, Jamesville-DeWitt School District; Corey Williams, Syracuse City School District; Benjamin Steuerwalt, Syracuse City School District; Rory Edwards, Syracuse City School District; and Meredith Devennie, Liverpool Central School District

**KEY TAKEAWAYS**

- Remember that an equity audit is a tool that shows where your equity gaps are. These gaps require addressing. The audit is a step toward making school more equitable, but just completing an audit does not result in greater equity.
- Build an equity audit team who will do the work of the audit together. This team is best composed of people with diverse backgrounds, experiences, and perspectives.

- Design the audit. Designing the audit includes determining the scope of the data to be collected (quantitative and qualitative), what variables or demographics you will use to analyze the data, who will collect it, and where the data will be stored.
- Collect the data for the audit. Collecting the data can be time consuming and labor intensive. Your school or district may or may not currently collect data by the demographic variables you need. Do not let that stop your audit.
- Analyze the data together. Too often teams skip this step. Making time to understand the data and make sense of it as a team is essential as you work to identify equity gaps.
- Make a plan for systemic change. Collecting and analyzing data does not create more-equitable schools. That comes from using the data to address the gaps illuminated by the audit.

This chapter is the product of a research-practice partnership between Syracuse City School District (SCSD), Jamesville-DeWitt School District (JD), West-Genesee School District (WGSD), and Syracuse University (SU) in New York state to engage together in the practice of equity audits. Coburn, Penuel, & Geil[1] define these partnerships as "long-term, mutualistic collaborations between practitioners and researchers that are intentionally organized to investigate problems of practice and solutions for improving district outcomes." This partnership consists of district-office leaders and university faculty focused on the Syracuse urban district and neighboring suburban districts where the administrators work and the university is located. We have engaged in this collective work over the last few years in the spirit that Cooper[2] argues knowing that research-practice partnerships are key to closing equity and opportunity gaps. Our team believes that equity audits are key tools to explore and make visible disproportionality and inequity—that is, to understand opportunity gaps—and are therefore a necessary step and driving force for creating more-equitable school policies and practices.

## DEFINING EQUITY AUDITS

Equity audits have become more commonly used tools in K–12 leadership preparation and equity-focused leadership practice. An equity audit[3] is a systematic examination of the practices of a school or organization to understand how educational equity is playing out: where there are gaps and where there is greater equity. This is a purposeful way to collect and examine data to provide a picture of how different states, districts, schools, and students are impacted by education policies and practices.

An essential part of this process is examining the experience of historically underserved or underrepresented populations. This requires disaggregating data using demographic and identity markers (e.g., race, class, language, disability). Capper, Young, & Frattura[4] describe this as anchoring equity in the idea of proportional representation. For example, proportional representation means understanding the number and percentage of Black students in advanced classes and comparing that to the local proportion of Blacks in the student population. If 30% of the student population is Black, we would expect to see that 30% of the students in advanced classes are also Black. If 10% of the students in advanced classes are Black, we have identified an opportunity gap because the proportion of Black students in advanced classes does not match the natural proportion of Black students in the school. Typically these audits examine proportional representation by using descriptive statistics and composition indices.

## ENGAGING IN EQUITY AUDITS

Learning from the work of various scholars,[5] we offer guidance to help others engage in the practice of equity audits and have structured this chapter around five key steps: building an audit team; designing the audit; collecting the data; analyzing the data; and planning for then making equity-focused change. For each of these key steps we explain what it means to complete that step and provide examples from our own audits.

### Building an Equity Audit Team

You want an equity audit to help move your school or district toward greater equity. Thus it is important that this is not the work of one person but rather a team effort. Building a cohesive and diverse team can help maintain momentum and promote sustainability. The size and scope of the audit can help determine who should be on the team. Capper, Young, & Frattura[6] provide guidance for school and district teams.

> At the school level, the team of no more than 8–10 individuals should include the principal and representative teachers, including special education, bilingual education, general education, support staff (e.g., school psychologist), and a community member associated with students of color at the school. The school should also have grade-level teams and one teacher from each of these teams should be on the leadership team. At the district level, the team should include a representative from each of the building leadership teams, though again, the size should be kept to about 10–12 individuals. The team should also include the

superintendent, director of special education, curriculum director, and at least one community member representing students of color in the district.

It is important to share both the focus of the work and the progress of the team with the broader school and district.

***Example from Our Team.*** Our equity audit team grew out of existing collaborative efforts between the Syracuse University School of Education and SCSD leadership. Several faculty from the school of education and key district leaders had been meeting for several months to share meals and ideas and build relationships, developing connections that led to many mutually beneficial collaborations. Both organizations provided seed funding to invest in two-year collaborative projects involving SU faculty and SCSD administrators or teacher-leaders to address key issues impacting the local schools. Building on a shared commitment to increasing equity in enrichment activities for students from historically underserved populations, our team embarked on a project to study the proportional representation of students in advanced academics, athletics, and fine arts. Given the areas under consideration, we needed partners with varying areas of expertise and access to data. Our group has expanded and shifted since then, but the initial audit team consisted of three SCSD administrators, two SU faculty, and a doctoral candidate. The two university faculty had expertise in inclusive special education and educational leadership. One was also a parent in the district. The SCSD team included the assistant superintendent, the supervisor of fine arts, and a district data analyst. As the project expanded, a teacher on special assignment and focused on athletics (now promoted to the director of athletics), joined the team, streamlining access to athletic rosters. Two of our original team members have since taken leadership positions with neighboring districts. Rather than disbanding our team, we have expanded to consider issues of equity in both urban and suburban districts and have added a new supervisor of fine arts.

The team is small enough in size to be nimble and efficient but large enough to maintain momentum and ensure that no one person is responsible for keeping the project moving forward. Each member of the team brings unique perspectives, skills, and talents to the group—some have expertise in qualitative methods while others are fluent in statistical analysis. Of particular importance, the district partners have access to the data necessary to engage in the audit and the spheres of influence to recommend and enact changes based on the data. Any of the districts could have done an equity audit without SU but our partnership provided purpose, accountability, and space with which to do it.

## Designing the Audit

Scholars have used equity audits in diverse schools and districts and in rural, suburban, and urban contexts[7] as well as both secondary and elementary schools. For example, Bleyaert[8] investigated equity audits used by five high schools working toward math curriculum mandates, and Brown[9] used equity audits in a systemic examination of dozens of elementary schools. More recently, Green[10] employed equity audit tools to create a community-based audit to support equitable school-community relations.

Far more often than for research studies, equity audits have been used as a practical tool in educational leadership. Additionally, across the country a variety of educational consultants and not-for-profits do equity audits for school, district, and state educational systems. Thus while the scholarly field has used and continues to use equity audits in research, it is more often an applied tool for practicing school leaders.

We recommend the comprehensive audits provided in the following books. These audits cover a wide range of data and equity issues and include perspectives that many leaders typically overlook. All three of these resources are geared toward equity-focused leadership.

- Frattura, E. M., & Capper, C. A. (2007). *Leadership for social justice: Transforming schools for all learners.* Corwin Press.
- Radd, S., Generett, G. G., Gooden, M. A., & Theoharis, G. (2021). *Five practices for leading equity focused school leadership.* ASCD.
- Theoharis, G., & Scanlan, M. (Eds.). (2020). *Leadership for increasingly diverse schools.* Routledge.

We recommend taking the time to dig into a comprehensive equity audit. This might include collecting all of the data suggested in the resources listed above. It is reasonable that you might take a full year to collect data. That said, there may be times when your team decides to do a focused audit. For example, we worked with a district that completed a focused, special-education equity audit looking at the range of service delivery, demographic, placement, and achievement data around special education. Regardless, your team should outline the scope and parameters of the audit by deciding what questions are being addressed, what data are being collected, how the data will be stored, and who will collect which parts. Theoharis & Scanlan[11] make the following suggestions for designing an audit.

> [First], we suggest considering these questions: What is the timeline for collecting data? What is the scope of the audit? What data should be collected? Will you do the entire audit? If not, why not? What parts will you focus upon? Why

not the other parts? Will you do some parts now and some parts next semester or year? What caused you to choose the data that you did? What reasons or rationale did you use? Why do you think these data are more important and other data are less important?

Second, think through the data collection for each piece of the audit before beginning, be methodical in the approach, and clear about defining the parameters ... [Make sure] to decide on who is responsible for collecting which pieces of the data, as well as naming protocols for data files, and where and how the data will be stored.

***Example from Our Team.*** We knew we were interested in opportunity gaps, identifying areas of inequity, but we needed to narrow our focus to make the project manageable and actionable. We decided to focus on three key areas: participation in athletics, in fine arts, and in advanced academic courses. We knew that access and opportunity gaps in advanced classes can be key gatekeepers for high school students in determining post-secondary success. Research is also clear that performing arts and athletics are important areas to consider in terms of identifying meaningful opportunity gaps since these activities provide a myriad of developmental benefits for adolescents[12] that correlate with positive academic, social, and emotional outcomes. Once we identified the three core areas under consideration, we had to define the scope of the audit. Were we going to look at data for all grades? How were we going to define participation? What specific activities fit within our parameters? After much deliberation we decided to focus specifically on data for students in grades nine through twelve in all of the district high schools. We defined participation in athletics as being a member of any extra-curricular sports team at the modified, junior varsity, or varsity level. For the area of fine arts, we made the decision to collect data on performing arts groups that were not required classes. In other words, participation in general music did not fit our inclusion criteria but enrollment in the orchestra did. We also included all extra-curricular music and theater productions. We spent the longest time deciding how to define advanced academics and what courses would we count for this designation. In the end we considered a class advanced if it led to a weighted average. This included dual enrollment courses with several local universities, International Baccalaureate, and Advanced Placement courses.

Once we had identified all of the opportunities that met our inclusion criteria, we developed a master index: a list of all the possible courses that met our criteria for advanced academics, sports teams, and performing arts groups or opportunities. We also needed a participation roster, which was a database of all students who participated in any of the opportunities in the index, and a demographic roster—a database with all the high school students for that academic year and their demographic information.

## Collecting Equity Audit Data

Once you have a plan for the equity audit, it is time to collect the data. It is important to be organized. This means having the data clearly labeled and in a location accessible to all members of the team. It is important to establish a clear and consistent naming protocol for all files so every member of the team knows how to save and access the data. You also need to establish and secure private electronic storage for all records as you are working with student data. Regular check ins with the team from members responsible for collecting pieces of data provides an important role in keeping the audit moving. Remember that data collection can take months or even an entire year. Theoharis & Scanlan[13] provide a couple of reminders about equity audit data collection.

> Remember: 1) data systems are only as good as the information in them, 2) different data systems do not always integrate information across platforms, and 3) not all information needed will be easily accessible. This often means that some of the audit will need to be completed "by hand." This is time consuming and labor intensive. Sometimes discovering these spaces within the school and district data can provide insights about data collection/storage improvements.

*Example from Our Team.* Gathering the data was more challenging than we initially expected. We had all of the right players at the table but much of the data was not available in an easily accessible form. For example, athletic rosters were created by coaches and stored as hard copy in file cabinets. These rosters were often inaccurate with incorrect spelling of names and missing student identification numbers—and many had never been filed with the appropriate office, requiring us to track down individual coaches and athletic directors. We then painstakingly typed each student name into our database, often having to do detective work to determine who the student was given the misspellings. We pored over programs for school musicals and hand-entered student names into our database. We were able to access electronic rosters for the academic classes as those were managed through a data system, but even there we found errors: classes that hadn't been coded correctly or courses with differing designations at different schools.

The work of hand-entering those names into the database was laborious and, at times, frustrating. When we began this audit, we quickly learned neither arts nor athletics were tracked via the electronic student data management system. It was our collective time sitting together, hand-entering data, sharing our outrage over the misspelled names, finding errors in the designations of advanced classes, and sharing our fears of what this might mean for specific students that led the district to create a mechanism to keep track of arts and athletics in the student data management system and to correct the recording of advanced courses for all students enrolled.

## Analyzing the Data

Too often the analysis of data is rushed because we think the data speaks for itself. It is important to take time and look at the data, prepare various different representations to see what communicates the data most effectively, and fully discuss *all* of the data collected with the entire team and even a wider and more diverse group of stakeholders. Radd et al.[14] provides important reminders about preparing and sharing data.

> Make sure that each individual has access to the data you plan to discuss, keeping in mind two vital precautions: (1) you should not share private and/or individualized student data in this process; and (2) you need to consider your need, rights, and possibility of ensuring that the data you share will be handled properly. For example, if you prepare data summaries for participants to read prior to the session, can you be certain they will not share the information to other parties, or worse, the press? When you distribute data for review, think carefully about where it could end up and the consequences of that happening. Consider ways to share the data that allow those involved in the analysis process to review it carefully, but not use it beyond its intended purpose.

Data sharing should ensure time to first discuss what the data says and then make sense of it. We want teams to foreground their assumptions at this point in order to better unpack the data. Remember that this is where we often need to return to the idea of proportional representation that we shared in the definition of equity audits. Using demographics and proportional representation is a vital part of equity audit analysis. A key part of the analysis process is creating a list of the gaps and issues that the data shows.

***Example from Our Team.*** Data analysis was a lengthy and iterative process for our team. While the statistical analysis was done primarily by our data analyst, every member of the team contributed to discussions about different ways to make sense of what we were seeing. The most important part of the process was looking at the data together, seeing patterns, asking new questions, and deciding how to present the findings so that others outside our group would be able to see what we were seeing. For some questions, simple descriptive statistics told a clear story. This was almost always accomplished by comparing the percentages of students participating in advanced classes, arts, or athletics of a specific demographic group to the overall percentage that the group made of the general population and looking for proportional representation. Proportional representation is a key tool for this kind of audit.

More sophisticated tools such as composition indices and risk ratios also helped illustrate areas of disproportionality in more nuanced ways.

In general the statistics were not advanced but the important analysis came from sitting down and discussing what the data showed. For example at one meeting we spent the entire time just naming a disproportionality in the data of advanced class enrollment. For example, "It looks like while Black students in high school make up 52% of the student body, Black students make up 37% of the advanced classes" and "It looks like students who receive free and reduced priced lunch make up 73% of high school students and 54% of students in advanced classes." We spent another meeting looking at many different visual representations of the data, adjusting graph colors and types to determine which ones captured the data in the easiest and most accessible way. Once we had gone through this process, we were able to present the data to others.

## Planning For and Making Equity-Focused Change

Equity audits do not matter unless they raise consciousness that leads toward creating more-equitable schools. We caution you that while an equity audit is an important tool, it is not the final goal. We will not create more-equitable schools by completing an audit and then stopping. The purpose of engaging in a collaborative equity audit is to identify equity strengths and gaps. This can and should lead toward making plans to alter policy and practices to change disproportionate realities and then going back to data collection to keep track of our equity audit–produced progress or lack of progress.

Leading a process in planning for and making equity focused change requires using the data to identify focused and specific problems. Radd et al. suggests,

> We recommend you pause: Slow your thinking and sit with the challenge to hold a systemic view of inequity alongside the need to decide where and how to start . . . With that view, you can begin to identify *a problem*—taking a "What problem should we fix right now?" approach.[15]

We then use that specific problem to develop theories of action (TOA) to address that problem with specific steps and measurable goals. A TOA is a simple *If . . . then* statement. *If* we do this *then* we should expect these results. Often the *If* clause of an equity-based TOA will have multiple parts to contribute to changing a specific outcome.

**Example from Our Team.** From the outset, this was more than a research project. We weren't just interested in documenting inequity; we hoped to create more-equitable schools and improve outcomes for all students in our area. But increasing equity is a mammoth task, one that requires thoughtful planning, data-informed decision making, and engaging the necessary stakeholders. After our first round of data analysis and our visualization of the gross inequities in all three areas under consideration, our district partners took concrete steps to increase access.

For example, the audit led to focused change designed to increase advanced academic participation by underrepresented groups in the International Baccalaureate Program (IBP). This resulted in a policy shift from only allowing selected students to be part of the IBP—a long-standing practice that had resulted in students of color, low-income students, students with disabilities, and ELL students being underrepresented in the IBP. This shift moved all ninth and tenth graders into the IBP for those grades, ensuring that all students at this high school were taking advanced classes. In the area of athletics, seeing that so few students with disabilities participated in athletics, the district added and then expanded unified sports teams at three of their five high schools. Unified sports teams are inclusive athletic opportunities specifically designed to engage students with disabilities in sports with non-disabled peers. This is in contrast to Special Olympic sports that are intended for students with disabilities or traditional varsity sports. The supervisor of fine arts, a member of our equity audit team, engaged all drama teachers and drama directors in courageous conversations about disproportionate drama participation. The initial plan from these conversations was to engage in intentional recruitment of underrepresented students into drama. Each high school developed specific recruiting strategies to target students from underrepresented groups for participation in theatrical productions.

## CONCLUSION

Our team came to believe in the power of this equity audit work. Together we were focused on a very tangible product: collecting and analyzing data for this equity audit. Engaging in this audit took equity out of the abstract and grounded it in the concrete realities of our local community. We saw the actionable and material nature of the audit as important to sustaining the necessary, ongoing nature of these audits. The audit became a practical way for others to think about this one aspect of equity. In the face of the variety of equity issues that challenged our district, creating a concrete product that led to specific conversations and actions felt rewarding to our team. A desire to unearth inequity and then hopefully make positive changes to district policy and procedures were driving reasons why we started this project. Thus, given the specific and substantive changes the district was making, continuing to engage in this work felt potentially productive—again emphasizing the importance of engaging in collaborative equity audits.

Yet part of the unintended power of doing this work was discovering other places in district systems that needed attention. Our initial data gathering was messy and time-consuming, taking well over a calendar year to complete. We learned that incorrectly spelled names often impacted other items for students, including misspelled school awards or scholarships. We wrestled together with the feeling of how culturally irresponsible it is to misspell students' names in a racially and ethnically diverse district. In deciding which classes would count as advanced academic courses for the audit, we found that there were inconsistencies in how particular advanced classes were being recorded in the system for some students.

The granular level of our data efforts, student by student and experience by experience, was the reason we identified these other equally important issues, issues that would have gone undetected without this painstaking effort. For example, course catalogs were corrected and new data management tools were implemented for recording athletic rosters. These were not intended outcomes of this project but they led to concrete and important improvements. These improvements encouraged our team to continue to move forward together.

This team, with its focus on an equity audit, created a space in which to begin and sustain this work. Working together we pushed this time-consuming and difficult (in the process and results) project forward. Accomplishing the initial audit created space for hopeful steps toward greater equity and led toward additional audits. While this work was not easy, we see the equity audit as an essential and meaningful practice that should be continued as part of culturally responsive and socially just leadership.

## REFLECTIVE QUESTIONS

- What are your current practices concerning data? What data do you already collect, disaggregate, and discuss?
- Do you have a team that can serve as an equity audit team or will you need to create a team? How will you ensure there are diverse backgrounds and experiences on the team? Will you have someone on the team who is skilled with analyzing quantitative data (e.g., skilled in the use of Excel, R, or other quantitative analysis software)? Qualitative data?
- What resources have you consulted to support your design of the audit? What will be the focus of your audit? What issues are you trying to understand?

- What data will you collect? What is the demographic information you will use to analyze the data (e.g., race, SES, ELL status, special education, gender and sex, religion).
- What process will you use to make sense of the data?
- What process will you use to make a plan to address the gaps you find?

## NOTES

1. Coburn, C. E., & Penuel, W. R. (2016). Research-practice partnerships in education: Outcomes, dynamics, and open questions. *Educational Researcher, 45*(1), 48–54. https://doi.org/10.3102/0013189X16631750

2. Cooper, L. (2007). Why closing the research-practice gap is critical to closing student achievement gaps. *Theory into Practice, 46*(4), 317–324.

3. Capper & Fraturra, 2009; Capper, Young, , & Frattura, 2020; Green, 2016; McKenzie, Gunn, Agan, Bullock, & Herrera-Evans, 2020; Radd, Generett, Gooden, & Theoharis, 2021; Skrla, McKenzie, & Scheurich, 2009; Skrla, Scheurich, Garcia, & Nolly, 2004.

4. Capper, C. A., Young, M. D., & Frattura, E. (2020). Equity audits as the core of leading increasingly diverse schools and districts. In G. Theoharis & M. Scanlan (Eds.), *Inclusive leadership for increasingly diverse schools* (2nd ed.; pp 186–197). Routledge.

5. Capper & Fraturra, 2009; Capper, Young, , & Frattura, 2020; Green, 2016; McKenzie, Gunn, Agan, Bullock, & Herrera-Evans, 2020; Radd, Generett, Gooden, & Theoharis, 2021; Skrla, McKenzie, & Scheurich, 2009; Skrla, Scheurich, Garcia, & Nolly, 2004

6. Capper, , Young, , & Frattura, 2020.

7. Frattura & Capper, 2007; Green & Dantley, 2013; Skrla, McKenzie, & Scheurich, 2009.

8. Bleyaert, B. (2011). Is compliance "Trumping" mission? Findings from an equity audit pilot. *International Journal of Educational Leadership Preparation, (6)*4, 1–11.

9. Brown, K. (2010). Schools of excellence and equity? Using equity audits as a tool to expose a flawed system of recognition. *International Journal of Education Policy & Leadership, (5)*5, 1–12.

10. Green, T. (2016). Community-based equity audits: A practical approach for educational leaders to support equitable community-school improvements. *Educational Administration Quarterly, 15*(1). https://doi.org/10.1177/0013161X16672513

11. Theoharis, G., & Scanlan, M. (Eds.). (2020). *Leadership for increasingly diverse schools*. Routledge

12. Farb & Matjasko, 2012; Feldman, & Matjasko, 2005.

13. Theoharis, G., & Scanlan, M. (Eds.). (2020). Leadership for increasingly diverse schools. Routledge

14. Radd, S., Generett, G. G., Gooden, M. A., & Theoharis, G. (2021). *Five practices for leading equity-focused school leadership*. ASCD.

15. Radd, S., Generett, G. G., Gooden, M. A., & Theoharis, G. (2021). *Five practices for leading equity-focused school leadership* (p. 184). ASCD.

## REFERENCES

Bleyaert, B. (2011). Is compliance "trumping" mission? Findings from an equity audit pilot. *International Journal of Educational Leadership Preparation, (6)*4, 1–11.

Brown, K. (2010). Schools of excellence and equity? Using equity audits as a tool to expose a flawed system of recognition. *International Journal of Education Policy & Leadership, 5*(5), 1–12.

Capper, C. A., & Frattura, E. (2009). *Meeting the needs of students of all abilities: How leaders go beyond inclusion (2nd ed.)*. Corwin Press.

Capper, C. A., Young, M. D., & Frattura, E. (2020). Equity audits as the core of leading increasingly diverse schools and districts. In G. Theoharis & M. Scanlan (Eds.), *Inclusive leadership for increasingly diverse schools* (2nd ed., pp. 186–197). Routledge.

Coburn, C. E., Penuel, W. R., & Geil, K. (2013). *Research-practice partnerships at the district level: A new strategy for leveraging research for educational improvement*. William T. Grant Foundation.

Cooper, L. (2007). Why closing the research-practice gap is critical to closing student achievement gaps. *Theory into practice, 46*(4), 317–324.

Frattura, E. M., & Capper, C. A. (2007). *Leadership for social justice: Transforming schools for all learners*. Corwin Press.

Green, T. (2016). Community-based equity audits: A practical approach for educational leaders to support equitable community-school improvements. *Educational Administration Quarterly, 15*(1). https://doi.org/10.1177/0013161X16672513

Green, T. L., & Dantley, M. E. (2013). The great white hope? Examining the white privilege and epistemology of an urban high school principal. *Journal of Cases in Educational Leadership, 16*(2), 82–92.

McKenzie, K. B., Gunn, J. M., Agan, T., Bullock, C. J., & Herrera-Evans, A. (2020). *Community equity audits: Communities and schools working together to eliminate the opportunity gap, addressing the pandemic* (2nd ed.). McKenzie-Gunn Educational Consulting.

Radd, S., Generett, G. G., Gooden, M. A., & Theoharis, G. (2021). *Five practices for leading equity-focused school leadership*. ASCD.

Skrla, L., McKenzie, K. B., & Scheurich, J. J. (2009). *Using equity audits to create equitable and excellent schools*. Corwin Press.

Skrla, L., Scheurich, J. J., Garcia, J., & Nolly, G. (2004). Equity audits: A practical leadership tool for developing equitable and excellent schools. *Educational Administration Quarterly, 40*(1), 133–161.

Theoharis, G., & Scanlan, M. (Eds.). (2020). *Leadership for increasingly diverse schools*. Routledge.

*Chapter 4*

# Flipping the Script through Virtual Reality Perspective-Taking to Increase the Culture of Belonging

Wendy Morgan, SHIFT, and Heather McClure, University of Oregon's Center for Education Promotion

#### KEY TAKEAWAYS

- Unconscious bias is a categorization process we all use to make thousands of snap decisions daily, both good and bad.
- Immersive virtual reality can give teachers deep insight into the ways in which unconscious bias leads to a lack of belonging.
- Virtual reality provides a space where someone can practice, fail, and practice again until they have developed confidence to use new skills in real life.
- School and district leaders should hold facilitated meetings after a virtual reality experience, with reflective questions geared at triggering teachers to think about how they want to move forward, to take what they experienced, learned, and felt and begin to apply that in their interactions with students.

A new teacher has carefully prepared her lesson plan. When she enters the classroom, she does a quick scan of the room, noting that the students seem wary of getting another new teacher at this point in the year. As she begins her lesson, some students fidget in their seats; one hits his forehead with his hands in a show of frustration; another makes a show of looking at their watch. One student gets up from his seat, and another says, "This class is so dumb," followed by sniggers from other students. One mutters, "Haven't we learned this already?" as a siren sounds nearby.

This scenario is from a prototype that Wendy's business, SHIFT, created to see whether virtual reality (VR) could present a high-stimulus classroom experience for equity-focused teacher training. Teacher participants enter the VR scenario prepared to teach a mock lesson to a classroom full of disruptive student avatars. Heather's research team was able to measure participants' stress through brief, self-report surveys embedded within the VR program to which participants responded immediately before each of two VR classroom experiences. The second stress appraisal took place after the participants engaged in a three-minute mindfulness intervention embedded within the VR program, which was designed to support participants' stress de-escalation and healthy emotional and physiological regulation. At the conclusion of the two VR classroom scenarios, teachers participated in a one-on-one, 45-minute debrief about the experience. The debriefs helped them explore what they experienced. For some highly experienced teachers, the scenarios were emotionally triggering and reminded them of their most challenging and upsetting early teaching experiences with students who were not receiving the support they deserved. Teachers also described their realization of previous unconscious biases they might not otherwise have been aware of in their daily interactions with students.

During the debriefs, SHIFT staff asked the teachers to reflect on the actions they took during the VR experience and to identify the wording of comments they said "in the moment" that they would have liked to change, and they helped them discover the things they could do moving forward in their interactions with students once back in their actual classroom. The goal of the debrief was to lead each teacher to discover what they could address in their behavior rather than have the facilitators tell them what they thought participants needed to change. After the debrief, the teachers taught the lesson in the VR scenario again, focusing on being less reactionary and more thoughtful in their interactions with the disruptive student avatars.

In this chapter we will discuss what drove us to this work and how we feel VR can be a tool in combatting unconscious bias. We will end by offering some implementation advice for education leaders interested in trying out VR to build empathy among teachers and a sense of belonging for students. As you read, contemplate the ways in which society has moved toward a greater reliance on virtual spaces, whether during a pandemic, as entertainment, or as a way to foster connectedness and work toward greater self-awareness and responsiveness.

## SO, WHAT IS UNCONSCIOUS BIAS?

Unconscious bias is a categorization process we all use to make thousands of snap decisions daily, both good and bad. For teachers, many of these judgments are related to student behavior in the classroom and evaluations of which behaviors warrant discipline and what kind of discipline. Studies suggest that unconscious associations about students, especially when the individual is under stress, can cause teachers and other school staff to make inequitable decisions about the type and severity of the discipline required. Studies show that these decisions can result in certain groups of students being more harshly disciplined than others. Disparities in the use of school discipline—in the form of out of classroom or out of school exclusion—by race, gender, ability, or sexual orientation have been well-documented[1,2] and continue to place large numbers of students at risk for short- and long-term negative outcomes. Students suspended from school miss out on instruction, are less likely to graduate on time, and are more likely to repeat a grade, drop out of school, or become involved in the juvenile justice system.

Our work and research have led us to believe that unconscious bias—that is, the attitudes or stereotypes that affect our understanding, actions, and decisions especially when we are tired, hungry, or stressed—is a compelling explanation for the continued presence of societal inequities in our school system and beyond. The persistence of disproportionate discipline, even among populations with equity-minded intentions, led us to the conclusion that more work is needed to recognize and mitigate the causes and instances of unconscious bias. In line with federal guidance, it is clear that more should be done to "enhance staff awareness of their implicit or unconscious biases and the harms associated with using or failing to counter racial and ethnic stereotypes."[3] Importantly, research also shows that through heightened awareness of our own internal state (e.g., stress level, hunger) and external conditions (e.g., disruptions) that make each of us more likely to make decisions informed by unconscious bias (referred to as "vulnerable decision points"), we can proactively reduce our stress and reactivity[4]—as we achieved in our early VR scenario with teachers by engaging them in a series of mindfulness exercises—thus reducing our likelihood of acting on negative stereotypes.

## SO, WHAT EXACTLY IS VIRTUAL REALITY ANYWAY?

VR is "an artificial environment which is experienced through sensory stimuli (such as sights and sounds) provided by a computer and in which one's actions partially determine what happens in the environment."[5] In a broader sense, VR includes interactive video gaming, virtual environments, and, commonly, multisensory experiences. VR uses many different technologies: monoscopic or stereoscopic displays, user tracking technologies, or augmented reality (AR) to merge real and virtual worlds.

Due to VR's combination of a high degree of control with ecological validity, it has been used as an effective treatment approach in different areas of the health field. VR has been used for rehabilitation (including neurorehabilitation after brain trauma); promoting emotional well-being in patients; encouraging rural teens to stop smoking;[6] reducing adolescents' pain during burn wound care;[7] and treating phobias, post-traumatic stress disorder, obsessive-compulsive disorders, attention deficit, cerebral palsy, and autism spectrum disorder.[8] VR approaches (e.g., role playing and multi-person facilitated chats) also have been used to increase social skills and social cognition[9] (such as, in our example, heightened awareness of vulnerable decision points when teachers are more likely to act on implicit biases).

## VIRTUAL REALITY AS A WAY TO FLIP THE SCRIPT

As we began to think about how VR could be used to counter disproportionate discipline in schools, we quickly came to the conclusion that teachers shouldn't just expect students to "try harder" to fit in to classroom norms, especially in the face of unconscious bias working against them. This emphasis came from our recognition, as Brené Brown describes it, that creating contexts for students to fit in does not equal belonging. "Fitting in is about assessing a situation and becoming who you need to be to be accepted. Belonging, on the other hand, doesn't require us to change who we are; it requires us to *be* who we are."[10] To promote educators' capacity to foster greater belonging, we set out to create an impactful experience that would lead teachers to work to change *their* behavior. As Wendy describes,

> It comes down to who has the power. Students experiencing bias don't have the power in the classroom, they are not even in a position of choosing to be in school. If you've ever walked into the wrong bathroom, that moment of embarrassment, it's an immediate sense of "I don't belong here." Students who don't feel a sense of belonging at school live with that feeling all day, every day. They

walk into a classroom and instantly have that gasp of knowing they are in a room where they don't belong.

Teachers have the power to make a difference, to flip the script, to set a tone for creating a culture of belonging so that a student walks in the door and feels they belong. Of course dismantling systemic bias, not to mention outright racism, is much more complex than a single teacher creating a sense of belonging, but starting there can have a huge impact that ripples out.

The VR scenarios SHIFT has created give the background of who the participant is embodying beforehand and then, once the participant is in the VR experience, everything the participant sees and hears is from that embodied person's perspective. In order to really be able to capture what the embodied avatar might be feeling, there is an internal monologue during the scenario. This enables the participant to hear both what the person they are embodying says to the people in the scenario as well as that person's unspoken thoughts. In prototype testing, we found that the conflict between internal monologue and what is said really brings it home to the participant how difficult it is to get through society when you're continually faced with bias—unconscious or not—and what you wish you could say out loud but can't because of the negative consequences you know will result if you do speak your mind. The internal monologue turns the VR experience into a perspective-taking that brings out empathy rather than just eliciting sympathy for someone's situation. The idea is that you can't really know what someone's life is like and how hurtful it is to be bombarded with bias just by watching a clip or doing diversity training. VR enables you to actually spend a few minutes being immersed in someone else's life experience.

From an initial classroom scenario, SHIFT created an eight-week, online Understanding Belonging course that culminates in a VR experience aimed at increasing empathy. The online components are coupled with a facilitated group meeting—a guided discussion of self-discovery of the realizations the participant has about their unconscious biases in professional as well as personal interactions. For example, one person who went through the program identified bias in how he interacted with unsheltered people. He reflected that when he walks to work, one route takes him past people who are living on the street, and he began to examine his internal reactions to walking through that area. After just a ten-minute VR experience, he had a new understanding of how it might feel to be treated inhumanely, and he began to intentionally walk that route to interact with and treat those people who were living on the street in a more humane manner, striking up a conversation rather than rushing past and averting his gaze.

## IMPACT OF VR

> The first time I took my own VR, I started crying. I had no idea it felt like this even though I wrote it. Feeling it, you literally experience it. It's just mind boggling.

Wendy's reflection above speaks to the power of the immersive VR experience. When we reflect on the work we've done so far, we recognize that the VR scenarios have several benefits. For one thing, participants can be geographically dispersed as long as they have access to the technology. A school or school district can offer the experience to staff in a self-paced approach rather than asking all to attend training on the same day. And rather than compelling participants to be vulnerable in a group setting, VR offers a safe space: you might get jarred out of your comfort zone, but it is in the safety of your own room, with the door closed, where you can really examine your actions and behaviors without judgment and without the trap of becoming defensive or trying to justify your actions.

VR provides a space where we can practice, fail, and practice again until we have developed confidence to use new skills in real life. While professional development seminars sometimes feel artificial, immersive VR scenarios create highly memorable, impactful experiences. VR isn't a silver bullet to end bias, but one study found that participants were 200% more likely to apply the skills they learned in VR compared to skills learned through in-person training.[11]

In addition, the level of vulnerability VR participants feel, and the depth of what they will share in a facilitated meeting after an immersive VR experience, can be astounding. For example, we had a participant in a management role who had a staff member with whom every interaction they had, verbal or written, always deteriorated in the same manner. The supervisor went through the Understanding Belonging course, and halfway through the course, she started realizing some of the reasons that their interactions never got any better. By the end of the course, she was able to flip that relationship and have productive communications with the staff member because she was taking that person's perspective and had gained a better understanding of where the other person was coming from. We had someone say, "This is the most safe place I've ever been where I could be extremely uncomfortable." The *A-ha!* moments are brought on when participants realize they had no idea how much rejection and pain unconscious bias can cause.

## IMPLEMENTATION LESSONS LEARNED

When we began working in the VR space, it was easy to be overwhelmed by all of the different scenarios where vulnerable populations experience bias. If the key to the impact of VR experiences is authenticity, it was daunting to envision the innumerable situations we might need to depict to address bias. What we've discovered, to our surprise and delight, is that two scenarios that we used with teachers that had nothing to do with teaching still had the desired impact. Teachers experiencing VR based on a healthcare scenario, for example, reflected afterward that embodying a patient who experienced a series of micro-aggressions helped them relate to what it must feel like for a student who experiences a lack of empathy from powerful adults. The vividly immersive VR scenario enabled these teachers to see that some students enter their classroom with a range of deep traumas. Students may be acting in a certain way because the world around them is hostile.

After experiencing an immersive VR scenario, it is important to hold a facilitated meeting with reflective questions like "How did you feel when you were there?" "What were your emotions?" and "Why do you think you had those?" The questions should be geared at encouraging the participant to think about how they want to move forward, to take what they experienced, learned, and felt and begin to apply it in their interactions with students. It is helpful to discuss a range of behaviors that the participant can modify; for example, verbal communication, written communication, and body language. Another aspect to consider is how the participant might develop their skill in recognizing the impact of their own behavior and acknowledging the authentic experiences of students. The individualized nature of the experience means that school leaders shouldn't expect teachers to immediately change how they interact with students, but when they incorporated mindfulness, incremental changes can lead to students feeling a new sense of belonging in schools. The mindfulness exercise that we use is Stop, Breathe, and Think. In a classroom situation when a disruption occurs, the teacher is stressed, and if a student starts yelling, the teacher may automatically respond by raising their voice, thereby escalating the situation. A VR perspective helps the teacher stop, breathe, and then think, "Why might the student be acting that way? What can I do that will de-escalate this?" The teacher begins to consider the trauma this student might bring with them into the classroom, asking, "Why might they be doing that? What trauma did they bring? What triggers are happening here for this student? And what will trigger them more or help de-escalate it for them?" We've found that the process may take months, with teachers going back and pulling out pieces of what they've learned, tools that they've been wanting to try. The content matures as the participants begin to apply it and intentionally expand on what they've learned. Participants report back that the VR gets under their skin in lasting ways.

A piece of advice: Schools, or school district leaders, should lead by example by engaging in the VR themselves. We have seen VR interventions fail if the administration brings in a program and says, "This is great, you guys go do this," but then the teachers ask questions that the leaders can't answer because they haven't done the training themselves. Buy in will evaporate if teachers think, "Wait a minute, if you don't care and you're not going to do it, why should we give it our all?" The role of the school leader is to facilitate change at the system level. It's the philosophical side of it: we do what we see others doing. If we're driving down the freeway and everyone is going over the speed limit, we're more likely to do that too, but if we notice other people are driving within the speed limit, we unconsciously do too. So administrators have to reward and highlight drivers of change, in staff meetings and in the ways they interact with staff. If they just take the role of monitoring change—walking the halls saying, "You have to go the speed limit"—teachers are going to keep speeding by.

Teachers can also make students aware of their efforts, and then it can be a classroom journey. Ultimately the VR experience is a personal journey but it helps if everyone involved—leaders, teachers, students—have a common language, shared goals, and ideas to talk about.

## FINAL THOUGHTS: NEW DIRECTIONS

In trying to create a VR scenario that would have the most impact in a school setting, it began to feel daunting to us to try to create internal monologues for the students that participants would embody. As SHIFT trialed a range of scenarios with different adults, we began to move in a new direction. Human beings are uniquely capable of giving inanimate objects emotion and affiliating themselves with an inanimate object. For example, there's a video of a circle and triangles, and the triangles keep bumping into the circle and the circle starts getting squished down. By the end of the video, people feel real empathy for the circle though it's still just a circle.

So now we have an idea to build a scenario where the participant is a shape in a competition with other shapes and the participant is supposed to do a series of tasks but the tasks are completely impossible for them because of the shape they are. Meanwhile the other shapes can complete the tasks because the tasks were designed for their shape. This seemingly simple experience can bring about a feeling of utter frustration from the inability to move along an expected path and trajectory simply because of the shape we happen to be. Participants are immersed in an experience of unjust bias without putting any labels on what group is experiencing the bias; it's just getting back to the holistic, overarching human need to be able to belong and function in the society we find ourselves in.

The impetus for this new direction comes from trying to figure out how to get people to not put themselves in a defensive box of thinking, "Oh, well that's not my bias," or "That's not something I ever encounter." The idea is to remove all of the potential objections that someone might have to what they're learning and experiencing. When we remove all human traits from the embodiment, the brain will still affiliate with the circle, feel emotion for it, and want it to succeed.

## REFLECTIVE QUESTIONS

- Who would embrace using a technology-based intervention like VR in your context? What would it take for that person to be a VR champion?
- What barriers are there in your context to engaging in an intervention that includes individual, self-paced moments coupled with group reflection?
- What other efforts has your organization undertaken aimed at creating a shared sense of belonging? What helped them stick? What caused them to erode?

## NOTES

1. See for example, Krezmien, Leone, & Achilles, 2006.
2. Wallace, Goodkind, Wallace, & Bachman, 2008.
3. Lhamon & Samuels, 2014, p. 17.
4. McIntosh, Girvan, Horner, Smolkowski, & Sugai, 2014.
5. Mesa-Gresa, Gil-Gómez, Lozano-Quiles, & Gil-Gómez, 2018.
6. Woodruff, Edwards, Conway, & Elliott, 2001.
7. Hoffman, Doctor, Patterson, Carrougher, & Furness, 2000.
8. Parsons, Rizzo, Rogers, & York, 2009.
9. Kandalaft, Didehbani, Krawczyk, Allen, & Chapman, 2013.
10. Brown, 2010.
11. PricewaterhouseCoopers, 2022.

## REFERENCES

Brown, B. (2010). *The gifts of imperfection: Let go of who you think you're supposed to be and embrace who you are.* Simon & Schuster.

Hoffman, H. G., Doctor, J. N., Patterson, D. R., Carrougher, G. J., & Furness, T. A., III. (2000). Virtual reality as an adjunctive pain control during burn wound care in adolescent patients. *Pain, 85*(1–2), 305–309.

Kandalaft, M. R., Didehbani, N., Krawczyk, D. C., Allen, T. T., & Chapman, S. B. (2013). Virtual reality social cognition training for young adults with high-functioning autism. *Journal of Autism and Developmental Disorders, 43*(1), 34–44.

Krezmien, M. P., Leone, P. E., & Achilles, G. M. (2006). Suspension, race, and disability: Analysis of statewide practices and reporting. *Journal of emotional and behavioral disorders, 14*(4), 217–226.

Lhamon, C. E., & Samuels, J. (2014). Dear colleague letter from the U.S. Department of Justice and the U.S. Department of Education. www2.ed.gov/about/offices/list/ocr/letters/colleague201401-title-vi.pdf

McIntosh, K., Girvan, E. J., Horner, R. H., Smolkowski, K., & Sugai, G. (2014). Recommendations for addressing discipline disproportionality in education. OSEP Technical Assistance Center on Positive Behavioral Interventions and Supports.

Mesa-Gresa, P., Gil-Gómez, H., Lozano-Quilis, J. A., & Gil-Gómez, J. A. (2018). Effectiveness of virtual reality for children and adolescents with autism spectrum disorder: An evidence-based systematic review. *Sensors, 18*(8), 2486.

Parsons, T. D., Rizzo, A. A., Rogers, S., & York, P. (2009). Virtual reality in paediatric rehabilitation: A review. *Developmental neurorehabilitation, 12*(4), 224–238.

PricewaterhouseCoopers. (2022). Blind spots. https://www.pwc.com/us/en/about-us/blind-spots.html

Wallace J. M., Jr., Goodkind, S., Wallace, C. M., & Bachman, J. G. (2008). Racial, ethnic, and gender differences in school discipline among US high school students: 1991–2005. *Negro Educational Review, 59*(1–2), 47.

Woodruff, S. I., Edwards, C. C., Conway, T. L., & Elliott, S. P. (2001). Pilot test of an Internet virtual world chat room for rural teen smokers. *Journal of Adolescent Health, 29*(4), 239–243.

*Chapter 5*

# Equity in Action

## *Efforts and Challenges of Recruiting and Retaining Teachers and Leaders of Color in Our Schools and Districts*

Gustavo Balderas, Beaverton
School District, Oregon

### KEY TAKEAWAYS

- The workforce in American schools still does not reflect the students served. It is critical to take intentional steps to recruit and retain school and district leaders of color. Affinity groups can provide the often-missing support that they need to thrive.
- Student advisory groups are an effective way to incorporate student voice in school policies and practices. It is important to ensure that participating students represent backgrounds that are proportional to the school population.
- Equity work in schools means ensuring opportunity, access, and inclusion so that every individual feels that they belong.
- Having a clear definition of what equity means and having not only all staff but students and community understand the term with clear examples of outcomes makes a clear statement for the need to focus on equity work within a school district.

- Use equity as the lens to develop initiatives and form budgets, both of which become moral documents for school districts and the broader community.

Our upbringing shapes who we are as adults. Childhood experiences can have a dramatic impact on how one feels about specific topics or situations as an adult and shape our perspectives, both personal and professional. At times our experiences bring back great memories and at times experiences bring back memories that are damaging upon reflection. My upbringing truly made an impact on me and continues to shape my views in both my professional and personal life and has strengthened my core values and my beliefs around my work involving equity.

I was raised in the small eastern Oregon community of Nyssa, a rural farming community of Mexican migrant families and White and Japanese farmers. My parents and entire extended family on my mother's side of the family settled in eastern Oregon when I had become ill as a newborn in Washington State, my birth state, as my family worked the strawberry-field season in the Mount Vernon, Washington, area. They settled for the long winter and never left this small town. My parents and extended family were migrant workers from Cahuilla, Mexico, and traveled what was called the agricultural triangle. The agricultural triangle was known to migrant working families from Mexico as a work path that followed the crop-growing seasons along the West Coast. We started off in California, working the fields in the California Central Valley and worked our way up to western Oregon and western Washington before heading back through eastern Oregon and western Idaho to finish up the root crops before making our way back to Mexico.

My family settled in a labor camp in Nyssa that was previously used as a Japanese internment camp. The camp had outdoor plumbing and felt like its own little town with some folks selling grocery items out of their home. It seemed that all the people who lived there were from either Piedras Negras, Mexico (where my family was from), or from across the border in Eagle Pass, Texas. All the folks were migrant workers trying to make money before returning to Mexico or Texas. I learned English in Nyssa public schools, there being a pullout program that back then meant learning phonics in a hallway with an instructional assistant and other Latino migrant students. As a youth I stuttered severely, something that made me deathly afraid to speak in Spanish much less try and communicate in English. This led me to be very introverted in my youth, and to this day I consider myself very much an introvert. As time passed, I learned English, and I was able to control my stuttering (although I still stutter on occasion to this day but have learned little tricks to hide it). After my parents settled in Nyssa, they moved out of the labor camp and eventually moved into a house in the community in which my mother still resides, a very small home that I still call home.

The one person I so strongly remember in my youth was a teacher, Mrs. Dorothy Bivens, a primary grade teacher I had over a two-grade span. Mrs. Bivens made my parents feel respected when they came to the school campus and gained their trust. Although my parents had very few English skills, Mrs. Bivens made them feel as equals to other families. The school had a kind staff that translated during conferences and whenever there was a need to communicate with anyone who couldn't speak English. She made a dramatic impact on me, and her manner of caring for students and families stays with me to this very day.

These early times helped form me and the views on education that have carried on to my life's work to give back to a profession that has provided me with an opportunity to improve systems for students with a similar experience such as I had growing up. Your early years truly mold who you are and will be. I had the opportunity to work in Hillsboro, Oregon, for 19 years. While in the Hillsboro District I worked at all academic levels—elementary principal, middle school teacher, assistant principal, and high school teacher and counselor—before becoming a school superintendent. As I have had the opportunity to lead school districts, I have increased my knowledge in how systems operate and how best practices have afforded students and districts more success in student engagement and thus greater academic gains and behavior supports. I credit any success that I have had to the people I have been so honored to have worked with and to the mentors who have given me so much support.

## THE ROLE OF ALLIES

During my tenure in Hillsboro, I had a tremendous mentor, Carlos Perez, who was the deputy superintendent of the district and who helped shape my view of how a school system should work. As a young administrator, Carlos took the time to meet with me regularly for early morning coffee to answer questions and to provide input on specific topics. Those meetings were extremely beneficial to me as a young administrator, and I will be forever grateful. To this very day, I try and pay it forward to any young educator who needs any advice.

Carlos and I helped form the Oregon Association of Latino Administrators (OALA) with a small core group of Latino educators in 2002 with the goal of increasing the diversity of our educational workforce and to provide a safe space where educators of color could connect with each other, as oftentimes educators of color find themselves without like peers in their buildings. In

Oregon at this time there was the Minority Teacher Act of 1991 that required school districts to have teaching staff who were reflective of the student population they served. Although this was in the legislative books, very little was done to ensure compliance across the state.

Our group was formed to help diversify the work force in Oregon, and it made a substantial difference. With the help of allies, the organization has grown and is a well-known entity within the state and region. I always remember Carlos remarking on how school districts struggle with change because they are looking for the right fit in their educators and administrative staff—the "right fit" sometimes being code for looking like the broader community, the majority White teaching and administrative workforce that is still the case today in the United States. Forming OALA helped Oregon improve its workforce diversification efforts and has helped in educating school districts on hiring and promoting practices to truly use a more intentional, non-biased approach to hiring. OALA is now an affinity platform for the Latinx educational community in the state and a group that is called on by state organizations and government for feedback on policy and future legislation. Our mother organization, the Association of Latino Administrators and Superintendents, has been successful in helping prepare aspiring superintendents for the top seat in school districts for many years. These affinity organizations are needed to help in leveling the playing field for so many educators who do not understand how to navigate the hiring process or the certification process. I still hear stories of current aspiring leaders of color who feel that it is a struggle to get through the door to their first job as they sometimes have very little support from others within their specific school district or when applying to another school district. There is a sense that there are sometimes alternative pathways for some educators and administrators in some school systems due to whom they know in that specific school system.

Although OALA began as a thought in the minds of a few administrators, it was initially supported by the Oregon Department of Education and the Coalition of Oregon School Administrators. The support came as both in-kind and financial support. These allies allowed the organization to be sustained in its early formation, and it is now in its 19th-year of existence. Organizations and individuals of color need allies to continue efforts to meet the needs of all students.

One area in which OALA has been successful is in the formation of an aspiring administrative protégé program. This program is currently in its fifth year of existence and has had a dramatic impact on the staff that go through the program. Of the protégés who have gone through the program, several have found administrative positions. The program also serves as an affinity group in which group members create long-standing friendships and find peers they can connect with as they progress on their professional journey.

OALA has monthly meetings for members and one yearly conference. These regular meetings serve as a needed networking opportunity where members can learn from one another and support each other in a safe space. The conference serves as an opportunity to share best practices and to reunite with peers. The conference has grown year after year and is well attended and supported by state agencies and state associations. Along with the conference there are monthly meetings for members. These meetings create an affinity group and create a safe space for members from around the region where they can share experiences and ask questions or get advice from other leaders.

## LEADING WITH AN EXPLICIT EQUITY STANCE

I define equity work in our schools as intentional acts to ensure opportunity, access, and inclusion so that every individual feels that they belong. The system needs to have metrics to hold it accountable to the stakeholders it serves and needs to report those metrics in a transparent manner. The system has a moral obligation of accountability to the stakeholders. At times I do not use the word "accountability" but rather "moral obligation" as "accountability" invokes a negative reaction from some people. You sometimes must be careful of the local political context when using specific terminology. There are key trigger words being used right now for political purposes, words such as "equity" or terms such as "culturally relevant curriculum," that can be spun into a negative context when all the districts are trying to do is teach to state standards and use curriculum that meets the needs of the students the district serves. There are some school leaders across the country who have difficulty when using the term "equity" and must use other terms such as "inclusion" or "access" to help their community understand the intent of the work around equity. Defining equity is also often problematic as school districts and communities have difficulty understanding what "equity" really means. Having a clear definition of what "equity" means and having not only all staff but students and community understand the term while also having clear examples of equity in action and outcomes produced through equity work makes a clear statement for the need to focus on equity work within a school district.

Systems should use information to ensure that the school system is being held accountable to students and families so that they do feel that they belong. The sense of belonging is something that is not inherent to an individual. They need to feel that they are supported enough to feel a sense of belonging. Access, inclusion, and opportunity are many times one-way constructs, having the organization be the provider and the stakeholders in the system, whether the stakeholders be students, families, or school staff, making it a one-way delivery. Giving those stakeholders a sense of belonging makes the delivery a two-way construct. The stakeholders have their own opportunity to engage at their level. In my belief, this is where the issue of equity truly lies. Organizational systems are typically outward facing, making them a one-way endeavor, and they truly need to be a two-way model to truly engage those that we need to engage, especially those in our schools who have been traditionally marginalized by our current model, those students who come from poverty, those students who are non-native English speakers, and those who are specially abled.

As an example, in school districts there are times in which most communication and many other aspects of our school system are one-way, making the school district the provider of information, be it a community meeting, an online grade-check portal for families, or a newsletter communicating all of the great things happening on a school campus. This manner of communication makes it difficult for the system to truly understand the needs of the broader community from parents to students to patrons wanting to engage in the school district. Often this one-way manner of communication is difficult for families to access. There may be language issues or a lack of technology. Having a more intentional model in which an equity lens is utilized allows a school district to truly provide intentional two-way communication. In this manner, school districts have multiple ways in which to communicate with families, providing them with options in which the families feel that they can engage with the school system. An equity lens gives the district a way of understanding gaps in the current communication model and allows the system to improve the model.

In one district I led, we were very intentional in how we engaged our families through our parent-family communications. One way we did this was bringing our Latino parents into a school board study session and having them speak in their native language to our non-Spanish speaking school board. The school board wore translation earbuds and were translated to. My board president at the time mentioned that this was the most impactful meeting she had attended in her 12 years on the school board. Parents cried, board members cried, and authentic stories were told from the perspective of the users, the parents. I still remember this meeting as if it happened yesterday due to its impact.

Another example is having a superintendent student advisory group that is representative of the students that the school district serves. We have each comprehensive high school and our program that provides an alternative educational setting for students submit student names for consideration for the advisory group. What we are looking for is to have a proportional group of students who are reflective of the students that we serve in the district. In this case 53% of our kids are students from diverse backgrounds and 17% of the students are in special programs. We are intentional in the makeup to support a student voice that is authentic. Too often you have student advisors who are not reflective but are those students you would typically think of who would make up student leadership groups in the district, those who come from college-educated households and those from the dominant culture. We have monthly meetings with these students and the senior cabinet to discuss current issues and hear from students on improvement efforts that they have to offer. Also we have a separate monthly meeting to provide training for these students on leadership skills led by our cabinet. I have found that some of these students have not had much of a voice and am amazed by the growth that they make during the school year through the training and the confidence that is visible by the end of the school year.

People may be familiar with an image comparing equity and equality in which kids are trying to watch a baseball game and there is a high fence. In the "equality" visual, each kid gets one box: only the kid who is tall enough to see over the fence can watch the game. In the "equity" visual, the boxes are allocated according to height so that all of the kids can watch the game. There is another visual in which one of the kids is standing in a hole and is at a greater disadvantage than just being on flat ground. Having the boxes positioned in a way that enables all of the kids to watch the game is one frame of equity. Having the fence removed is another. Having the kids themselves play the game, yet another. A clear equity stance is needed to ensure access, opportunity, and inclusion so that others have a sense of belonging.

In the two situations I described above, the parents were given the opportunity to ensure that they had stronger access (speaking in their native language) to the school board, and students were intentionally selected to provide an equal voice in sharing their experiences. Equity work, like much other work, is not perfect and needs to be determined locally to ensure that it is sustainable. Having a framework and other tools to address situations helps a system in calibrating the work happening and the work that needs to happen.

In my tenure as an educator and leader, I have grown in my insights on how to best support our students and families. Having the right systems, the right culture, and the right accountability helps create an atmosphere for success. It seems simple enough from outside educational circles to see how this works but it can be difficult to accomplish inside a school district because school systems are controlled by adults in the system, and those adults, like many outside of school systems, do not like change. School districts and individual schools have their ways, the "Insert school or district name here" way, and that way is how things are done in the district or school and how they have been done for years. Any change to this impacts the specific system and can, or will, cause internal issues, both negative and positive. This causes equity not to be as visible as it needs to be. I have heard too often, "We tried that, but it didn't work" from district staff in districts I have led. My reply is always the same. Each year we have a new team of people within the school system so "We tried that" is not accurate since each year we have a new "We." Every year is truly a new start. School systems sometimes forget that they are here to serve their customers, and those customers are *all* students and *all* families.

One example is how a school district hires. Many systems have a specific hiring protocol that they have used for years without much review for improvement. When pushed, district leaders often state that they have "tried this" or "tried that" and that the current way is the best way to hire in the area. This is the curse of the "District Way," and there is little change that occurs due to people being very comfortable in processes that can become antiquated over time. By revisiting systems within a district periodically, on an intentional timeline with people assigned to the responsibility, a school district will improve their processes.

As school leaders we have a moral obligation to ensure that we are doing everything we can do for all our students and their academic and social emotional needs. As budgets get tighter and we deal with the unknown that comes to us, most recently the COVID pandemic that hit school districts in March 2020, we must adjust and be very fluid in how we operate. What we also know is that we must adjust our systems to ensure that those students and families who have been traditionally marginalized by our systems are given additional support to ensure that they are being supported to meet their needs. Every student needs to be able to be known by strength, name, and need regardless of their status. School districts need to be able to provide differentiated supports to meet the needs of every student and every family whenever possible. I will describe how as a team of educators we were able to lead very substantial changes in a system to support more students and close gaps between different groups of students in a university town through the implementation of equitable systems.

## EQUITY EFFORTS IN PRACTICE

The Eugene School District, or better known as 4J to the locals, is a mid-size Oregon school district located in the lower Willamette Valley. It is comprised of 16,000-plus students on 32 campuses in a university town. Although the community is the second-largest in Oregon, it feels much smaller. The community has an alternative vibe, and much of the community views itself as progressive. The school district had a lengthy teacher strike decades ago that led to a site-based decision-making model in which individual schools had a great deal of autonomy. This was good for its time but led to inequities throughout the system during current times as the demographics shifted. I will speak to those inequities and what the district did to address inequities that helped improve overall achievement and student engagement.

The board of directors hired me as superintendent of schools in the Eugene School District in the summer of 2015. When I interviewed, their goals for me were to align the system and to work on the implementation of best practice systems to ensure student needs were being met. The board understood that the school district was fragmented and that it needed to have better internal systems to create more successful outcomes for the students. As is typical for school superintendents, I provided my short-term plan to understand the school system and then come back to the school board with a plan of action. I quickly learned how disparate the schools were because of a lack of alignment to a common direction. The school board had the courage to understand what needed to happen and supported me as I made adjustments that provided for substantial changes in the school system to ensure that we were providing an equitable education to all students in our charge. We were able to adopt a solid strategic plan through a strong community process involving 54 people from throughout the community and our school staff. This plan helped frame our goals and became our north star. In Eugene, as in most districts, the process of developing this plan was as important as the final product. We sought great community input through both presentations and surveys. I felt that the broader community owned the plan.

The district was very intentional about who was on the strategic planning team. It was comprised of members from all regions in the community, from private industry to our own school staff. We had association presidents, board members, students, and parents who were all able to participate and contribute to the development of the plan. The team met monthly for six months, and the district took the draft plan to the broader community for feedback in regional meetings in multiple languages and then brought back the feedback and worked on any revisions. The process was led by an outside consultant who did a fantastic job of ensuring that all understood that the purpose of the committee was to bring forth recommendations to the school board for their approval. If the committee got stuck on a possible recommendation, the school board would decide on the language.

I believe that school districts can improve through the implementation of effective systems, providing a culture of success, and by holding the system accountable for the success of each student, by creating systems that are broad and impact every aspect of a school district from hiring practices to budget development to ensuring that there is clarity in the direction of the school district. Culture is the people within the system, having not only the right people in the right positions but also ensuring that there is the right professional growth and opportunities for those people. Holding a system accountable to its stakeholders, the students, and families it serves means transparency in data that is disaggregated to ensure all students' needs are being met.

One example of systems and accountability is ensuring that all high school students are on grade level and accruing the right amount of graduation credits needed each school year. This seems simple enough to do but harder in practice especially in larger districts with multiple high schools due to the uniqueness that high schools can have through specific program offerings. Some have International Baccalaureate Programs, some have lots of Advanced Placement classes, while others have a unique career program. But all have the same standard requirements that are provided by the state board. How a district achieves these credits is what makes it unique. This is shaped by the school schedule and calendar. Having quarter instructional periods versus trimester periods or having six-period days or four-period blocks makes a substantial difference in how many credits a student can accrue over time. Having a specific on-time graduation goal by grade level enables a school district to understand the needs of each student. If a district has a strong graduation goal, say expecting 95% of students to graduate on time, doesn't it make sense that that same goal be at every grade level once a student enters high school?

In my current district, students can gain six units each year toward the state-required 24 credits needed to earn a high school degree. The goal is to have a solid understanding each grading period, every quarter grading period in this case, of where kids are at and who is not on track and then to develop plans to help those students get back on track by the end of summer for that specific school year. If a ninth-grade student falls off track, we must develop a plan to get them on track by the end of their ninth-grade summer. If we do not do this, students can have a sense of failure due to having so much to catch up on that they leave our school system. These kids are pushed out by a system that is not systemic in having a personalized educational plan to support their needs. A school district needs data that are easily retrieved, a team that reviews data regularly, and the ability to provide supports to its students. If 95% of ninth-grade students are on track to graduate, a district should put in a strong effort to maintain this and work hard to ensure that the other 5% are caught up and supported. We have a moral obligation to all our students within our school system, an obligation to work each day to know every student by name, strength, and need.

Our district spent a great deal of time being very intentional in the hiring process. We were always on the recruiting trail and looking for the very best candidates who could add value to the school district. At the end of my five-year tenure, we had the most-diverse administrative team in Oregon and were second in teacher proportionality. We were always on the recruiting trail and all staff, and each board member, understood our goal and the rationale for our goal of diversifying the workforce. Students of color have a stronger connection to school behaviorally and academically if they have staff who are reflective of themselves. We recruited locally and statewide and were able to attract superb administrative talent to the school system. We supported our diverse administrative group through monthly affinity meetings and socials. We began a teacher mentoring program that provided support from master teachers and an opportunity to have a mentor of color if the staff member asked for this specific support. A school district must work just as hard at retaining its quality staff is it does in recruiting its quality staff.

All this work needs to be put through an equity lens, a decision-making series of questions that calls out the impact of decisions on specific groups of students. There are several equity lens tools out there for folks to use. What I have found during my tenure as a school superintendent is that school systems struggle with decision making. They often do not have a decision-making tree and struggle to understand how decisions are made and who is responsible for making decisions. Using an equity lens does not replace a decision-making tree but adds value to help the overall system understand the impact of those decisions on specific stakeholders. A decision tree helps the school system understand how the district makes decisions and who has responsibility; an equity lens provides information on the possible impact of decisions on specific groups of people.

An example of using an equity lens is in the review of our alternative program in Eugene. The program was housed at the local community college campus a few miles outside the city limits. Due to the location and the program not truly feeding into the community college as had been expected, the district had an opportunity to review program placement and program model as it looked to move the program off the community college campus. Some equity lens questions such as "Who benefits most by placing the program at this location?" and "Which students move out of our high schools and attend this program and why do they elect to attend this model of program?" provided great discussion and debate on the future of the program. What we found was that the high schools had a tendency to place students who were not successful on the high school campuses in the alternative school program. An unintended consequence of this was that these students were then dropped from their home high school roster as the alternative school had its own state school code. The graduation rates were inflated because kids not keeping up with their required credits were not on their home campus.

What we decided to do was to build a new, much smaller program on the property of the district office which was in the center of town and very close to public transportation. This provided an opportunity for students from all the regions to come to the center of town and not provide more of a deficit to students who lived very far away from the community college (I heard a story of a 90-minute public bus ride for a teen mom and her toddler with a bus transfer in between). We intentionally made the program smaller and provided additional staff to keep students at their home school for credit retrieval opportunities. We created the position of graduation coach at each high school to help support students who fell behind in their credits. And we provided additional structure and rigor at the alternative education campus, replacing the building leadership and some of the staff. All of this created a different intention for the campus, and the results followed: more students were on track and graduation rates went up, and more students were given an opportunity to stay with their peer group at their home school. An equity lens, a set of questions, allows a team to understand the issues and the impacts of decisions and helps guide a team to have a dialogue in an intentional manner.

## THE IMPORTANCE OF A FOCUS ON CULTURE

In the five years I had the honor to lead in the Eugene School District, the district improved graduation rates by 18% overall and closed gaps, improving our Black graduation rates by 31%, Latinx students by 27%, and our students in special programs by 29%. We did this by being very intentional in our actions. To begin our work, we assessed the leadership skills of our building leaders, many of whom had been in the school district for several years. We used data that was present, both student academic and behavioral information, and staff information, how many of the staff were new to the school or to education, to provide a snapshot of a school and the school leader. In that five-year period, we changed 90% of our building leaders and replaced all the central office leadership team. Some retired and some just needed to be in a different place in the school system. At the same time, we were able to replace building leaders with leaders who were more reflective of our school community. The why is simple. We were stagnating as a school system, lacking clarity in direction as a district, and not meeting the needs of our students. By changing leadership we were able to have building leaders with a common goal, a common direction, leaders who had ownership in achieving goals to support all students. This is not to say that previous leaders did not have goals, but leaders can become less effective after several years in the same position. Some in the community initially questioned why we were shifting leaders at a rapid pace. Once the community saw that the schools were improving, the questions stopped and people were happy with the movements made.

Forty percent of our building leaders were leaders of color when I left the school district to lead another, compared to the 10% that were there when I arrived. This is higher than the 30% of the student population that comes from diverse backgrounds in Eugene 4J and something that I feel made a substantial difference in the overall culture of the organization. System change truly begins with having the right leaders in place to lead at the building and district level.

How and why would a system go through so much change, some may ask. The change needed to occur to create the system that was needed for our students to succeed. The system had been stagnant in its approach to improving student achievement and in supporting students behaviorally. These changes happened with little pushback from the board or broader community. This also told me that the community was ready for a change. The only pushback I received was in working to diversify the leadership team. There are bodies of research that have found that students of color do better academically when they have access to school staff who look like them. I heard rumblings early in my tenure from the community about why I was replacing White leaders with leaders of color, something that I found fascinating. I do not feel that many people would ever question a White principal being replaced by another White principal. But when I replaced those leaders with leaders more reflective of the student population, I did get pushback early on. This pushback stopped when outcomes for students quickly improved.

The district was very aggressive in recruiting and promoting the right personnel. We had a laser-focused hiring and recruitment plan and enacted that plan with precision. The entire leadership team understood the goal and understood their role in achieving our objectives. The plan came from the strategic plan that was created and the goal of recruiting and retaining staff. I spent a great deal of time cultivating relationships and helping entice leaders from the outside to come to Eugene. Once we hired the personnel, we then had a laser-focus on keeping those people within the system. The retention plan is just as important or even more important than the hiring plan. We had mentors for licensed and administrative staff, and we tried to find affinity group mentors for our staff of color. Affinity group meetings were supported by the district. Our leaders of color met monthly as a group to discuss issues impacting them in a safe space and to have a dinner together. These meetings were informal, with no agenda other than bringing up problems of practice seen by the administrative group. People truly opened up on how they felt and what supports they might need as the group came closer together. This was a very impactful practice that the leaders appreciated. Through the implementation of an aggressive hiring system, the district was able to change the culture through the changing of building leaders to hold it more accountable to the students it served. In this case the graduation rate improved and was the metric used to show success. It truly is a theory of action approach, if you do $x$ then $y$ will or should happen.

Another area of substantial change occurred in aligning our instructional materials and alignment of our school schedules and calendars. Our staff created a curriculum adoption process involving strong community and staff input, and our school board adopted this process. The district had no formal adoption process in the past and had a great deal of teacher-created curriculum being the sole source of curriculum to match our required teaching to the adopted state curriculum standards. Teacher-created curriculum is fantastic if it is done intentionally and is aligned across grade bands and vertically across grade levels. However if done without much intention, it can create inequities in which some staff can be teaching to different standards and there are curriculum gaps within the school system. The end users, our students, are the ones impacted through this approach.

The district began a cycle of curriculum adoption during my tenure that was very intentional. We tried not to overburden staff by being mindful of which content area was being adopted, expanded our focus on ethnic studies curriculum, and added career and technical education pathways to engage more students across our secondary schools. We used a strong focus on purchasing culturally relevant materials in an aligned manner for the first time in the memory of the school district. The district previously had been very autonomous in its purchasing of materials, creating an imbalance within the school district as there was no alignment in what materials were used to teach specific curriculum standards. Some of the materials were also purchased through outside, parent-raised funding, adding another layer of inequity between schools. In some cases, there was also a lack of alignment between grade levels. The new curriculum adoptions provided all staff and students with a baseline of curricular materials that served as a baseline of materials that teachers could then augment as they saw fit. The students need to see themselves in the staff that works with them in our schools and in all material that the district provides.

Instructional minutes is an area that I feel provided one of the most substantial changes to provide an equitable education that we were able to implement in Eugene. Due to a tough winter in which we had to cancel school for several days, we did a deep audit of our instructional minutes to ensure we complied with state expectations for the minimally required instructional minutes. What we found was astonishing. Over a period of years due to the lack of centralized control of building schedules, there was a creation of a gap of seven months of instructional minutes kindergarten through twelfth grade if a student were to follow a specific school feeder path. This specific path impacted our students most in need, those students who came from diverse backgrounds, and those who qualified for the free- or reduced-meal program. This was an unintended consequence of a site-based system that allowed each school site to vote on the yearly calendar and the daily schedule that they wanted to follow. There were no centralized controls to put guard rails to the minutes from the district level and the outcome was something that needed to be addressed. We worked with our association partners to correct this situation and created a standard for each academic level.

High school scheduling was another area of focus. Students in the local area were typically not fully scheduled from their freshman year on. There were gaps in their schedules, sometimes gaps of two or more periods, in which they had no class scheduled. We worked to correct this and made it the expectation to fully schedule students up to eleventh grade, making allowances only for those in their senior year. We began to track students by grade and worked to ensure that all students were scheduled and on track by grade level. We hired graduation coach coordinators at each high school to help with the tracking of students. These folks developed relationships with those students struggling and were able to work with the high school counselors in providing support to the students. What you would expect, those students with the lowest graduation rates, our students from diverse backgrounds or in special programs, were the ones most likely to be off track for graduation. School districts need to be very intentional in how they support kids to ensure they know where they stand throughout their school experience and not just when they reach senior standing and find out that they need to earn additional credits during a short time frame to be able to graduate with their peer group.

## BEYOND ACCOUNTABILITY: A MORAL OBLIGATION

"Accountability" is sometimes a word that brings a sour taste to the mouths of people. It is a word that brings a sense that there is a specific standard that needs to be upheld to meet a performance standard. In education, we do not pick the students that come through our doors, and we need to do everything we possibly can to meet the needs of our students. As mentioned earlier, instead of the word "accountability" I use the term "moral obligation" as it is a core obligation to ensure we are meeting the needs of all of our students. We have a moral obligation to all our students. I strongly believe that a school system needs to have data sets to ensure that it is holding the system accountable to the students it serves. A system cannot hold the students more accountable than the adults within the school system. This is a system's moral obligation. Having the right data systems to be able to use information at the classroom and the district level is essential to ensure that schools meet the needs of the students.

First and foremost, the system needs to have a robust system in which data is stored in order to be used effectively and in a consistent manner. Whether it be attendance data, behavioral data, or academic data, all data needs to be able to easily be obtained to be used by staff throughout a school system. Staff need to be trained in how to use the data to make decisions through a systems approach at the classroom level to the board level, and data needs to be reviewed often and in a transparent manner. Once the data are reviewed, a response needs to come from the review. At the classroom level, staff should meet to review specific student data and make recommendations to help support individual students and their needs. At the district level, budgets are reflective of the needs of the students and staff and help support any extension or intervention needed.

The use of data is essential to ensure that every student is having their needs met. The use of data also allows a school system to spend money effectively, focusing on those programs that are working and doing away with those that do not work. Having a set number of initiatives, and not having initiative overload, helps a school system do a few things well. By doing a few things, it also supports the bottom line, the budget, and keeps the district focused.

## FINAL THOUGHTS ON EQUITY

"Equity" is often a misunderstood term. It is a buzz word that is being used widely in districts and schools. Understanding what "equity" means is confusing for people. I feel that school districts often struggle with understanding what equity means in action. What I described here is one person's perspective of the work done in one specific, mid-size school district around equity work, which is a district's daily work, and how the school district was able to make dramatic changes in a relatively short amount of time. Having the entire system understand how it defines equity, by having a strategic plan that focuses on key initiatives that focus on closing gaps between groups of students and staying the course on these initiatives and using data to measure the progress of both programs and students within programs, will cause the system to succeed. This has been a proven formula time and time again across the United States.

I urge school systems to follow what has been proven to be successful. With nearly 14,000 school systems in the United States, there are plenty of models to replicate. Use equity as the lens in which initiatives are developed and how budgets are formed because budgets are moral documents for school districts and the broader community. School districts need to continue to morph as the demographics change within the system. Being nimble is something that school districts have not been good at in the past. For our kids' sake, we need to be agile and adjust as our student populations have changed greatly over time. Being agile will cause more success for all our students. In the end, our students deserve for us to continue to strive to be as successful as possible.

## REFLECTIVE QUESTIONS

- How do you support migrant students and families in your school or district?
- How well do the faculty and staff reflect the students in your school or district?
- What can be done to ensure that more teachers and leaders of color are recruited and retained in our schools and districts?
- What does equity mean in your school or district? Do you have examples of positive outcomes of equity work?
- How can we encourage student voice in our schools and districts?
- How can the personal narratives of migrant students inform our practices as school and district leaders?

*Chapter 6*

# Culturally Responsive and Socially Just Leadership Practice

*Creating Inclusive Service Delivery*

George Theoharis, Syracuse University, Sarah D. Lent, Wisconsin Center of Education Research, and Kimana Kibriani, Syracuse University

### KEY TAKEAWAYS

- Inclusive education means creating culturally responsive and socially just schools where all students regardless of ability, race, language, or income are integrated and supported in general education.
- Services like special education and English as a new language (ENL) can and should be inclusive where students from all backgrounds and ability have access to general education curriculum receiving collaborative support of the school community to succeed.
- Leaders need to develop a bold vision of inclusive education to drive a process leading toward improving their service delivery.
- School leaders should bring staff together, provide direction, communicate, and democratically create an implementation plan for a more inclusive service delivery.
- Mapping out current service delivery in the form of visual representation of the classrooms and various services offered in pullout programs or self-contained classrooms gives everyone a complete picture of all the human resources allocated to students' needs.

- School teams should create a revised service delivery system that serves all students inclusively in order to match that bold vision of inclusive education.
- Leaders must invest in building instructional teams to collaborate and transform classroom practices.

The provision of special education services for the nearly 7 million school-age students with disabilities in the United States is driven and mediated by the Individuals with Disabilities Education Improvement Act of 2004 [IDEA 2004].[1] Nationally 63.5% of students with disabilities are in the general education classroom for 80% of the day or more. Only 17% of students labeled with intellectual disability and 48% of students receiving services under the label of emotional disturbance access general education for the same percentage of the school day.[2] The over-representation of students of color in special education represents an area in which complex intersections of race, class, and ability translate into marginalization and exclusion.[3]

The number of English language learners (ELLs) in schools has increased substantially in the last 40 years. In the fall of 2018, ELLs made up 10.2% of public-school students in the United States (5 million students) compared to 9.2% in 2010 (4.5 million students). Educational programming varies for ELLs across states as a national law such as IDEA for special education does not exist for ELLs. Programming can range from students receiving ELL services outside the regular education classroom for the entirety of the day, for periods of the day, or within the classroom. There is no evidence that removing ELLs from the classroom results in academic or social-emotional gains for students.[4] Students from language minority backgrounds are more frequently placed in lower ability groups and have higher dropout rates than those whose first language is English.[5] For decades Thomas and Collier[6] have documented that pullout ELL services are the least effective.

Inclusive services for students with disabilities is the most effective practice[7] and key to creating more just and equitable schools.[8] Likewise decades of compelling scholarship has shown that providing English as a new language (ENL) in traditional English as a second language (ESL) pullout programs—the kind the vast majority of schools use across the nation—is the least effective service model.[9] Again the intersections of race, class, and language translate into marginalization and exclusion for ENL students. We have witnessed a growing call for and use of inclusive ENL services.[10] With this empirical base in mind, school and district leaders wishing to create more culturally responsive and socially just schools need to be able to change current service delivery that too often leaves certain students excluded, pulled out, or removed from general education for significant portions or even the entirety of their education. A key leadership practice is to create more authentically inclusive services.

## DEFINING INCLUSION AND INCLUSIVE SERVICE DELIVERY

Inclusive education is "the valuing of diversity within the human community . . . abandon[ing] the idea that children have to become 'normal' in order to contribute to the world."[11] In practice, inclusive education is when students have access to the general education classroom "regardless of ability, race, language, and income [and] are integral members of classrooms, feel a connection to their peers, have access to rigorous and meaningful general education curricula, and receive collaborative support to succeed."[12] As students with disabilities have long been denied access to general education and historically excluded from opportunities to be included in school alongside their peers, inclusive education is a social justice issue for students with disabilities.

While the term "inclusion" is not mentioned in any education legislation, IDEA emphasizes public schools' responsibility to see that students with disabilities have access to the support they need to be successful in the general education classroom. While inclusive education has become an increasingly prevalent educational outcome, achieving this goal is deeply influenced by context, is connected to systems of marginalization, and is complex in and of itself.[13]

Creating inclusive service delivery models entails moving away from self-contained special education services where students are removed from the classroom for part or all of the day and providing services in the general education classroom. This implementation of a co-teaching model provides a more inclusive education than teaching in self-contained or resource (pull-out) classrooms. As is true for special education services, ELL services can and should also be inclusive. Two-way dual language models and co-taught ESL classrooms are leading inclusive service delivery models. These are departures from pull-out models where students receive instruction in a separate classroom either full or part time.

As we'll discuss later in this chapter, moving toward more inclusive service delivery models requires mapping out and identifying how students are currently receiving services in order to realign and make these shifts.

## LEADERSHIP PRACTICES IN CREATING INCLUSIVE SERVICE DELIVERY

Across areas of learning differences (special education, ENL, etc.) a key practice to creating more socially just and equitable schools is creating and maintaining inclusive service delivery. This chapter focuses on four key steps for creating inclusive services.[14]

- Develop a bold vision of full inclusion but engage in collaborative planning and implementation.
- Map current service delivery.
- Realign school and staffing structure based on that bold vision.
- Build instructional teams to transform classroom practice.

The remainder of this chapter explains each step and provides examples from leaders and teams engaged in this practice. The examples come from five different schools and a district with which we have worked across the United States. These span elementary through high school and include the Northeast, Midwest, and West Coast.

## DEVELOP A BOLD VISION OF FULL INCLUSION BUT ENGAGE IN COLLABORATIVE PLANNING AND IMPLEMENTATION

A strong leadership vision of inclusive schooling is vital for the successful implementation of inclusive practices. Leaders need to be visible and consistent in their vision to move toward fully inclusive schools. Successful culturally responsive and socially just leaders do not accept some segregation or partial inclusion as a goal nor do they talk in platitudes like "All children can learn." They are specific and firm in their vision for inclusive schooling, returning to it to drive planning and to make decisions for the school.

The leader facilitates the planning process in a democratic and transparent manner with a representative leadership team consisting of school administrators, general education teachers, special education teachers, and other staff members. Leaders provide direction and they bring staff together—special education teachers, general education teachers, support staff, and paraprofessionals—to figure out how the people in their school can make that happen. The planning and implementation need to be democratic.

*Examples.* We have seen leaders take different approaches to holding and articulating bold visions of inclusive services. One superintendent would say regularly that while they were an excellent district they needed to be increasingly inclusive of the students with the greatest needs: We have "an obligation to the students [with the greatest needs] to change our service delivery." She kept a Post-it note on her desk reminding herself of this.

Another district administrator team took the new leadership job description with which Causton and Theoharis[15] end their book about leading inclusive schools and made it into a poster for all administrators' offices. It encourages leaders to "include each and every child"; "foster belonging for each student; for each member of your staff, for each family"; and "be bold."

A school leadership team set goals they created to create more inclusive service delivery in three areas: 1. School structure—how we arrange adults and students; 2. Meeting the needs of all in general education; and 3. School culture. The assistant principal from this school commented, "We brought these goals to every meeting to remind ourselves where we were going and what we had committed to do." Here's a more detailed look at these goals.

### School Structure

- Students will be placed in balanced classrooms.
- A designated person will facilitate efficient monthly communication meetings for staff to discuss various topics surrounding inclusion.

### Meeting the Needs of All in General Education

- Hold planned opportunities for vertical communication to provide continuity between grade levels.
- Provide child-centered, differentiated, research-based instruction that challenges children of all abilities and is supported by targeted staff development.
- Engage in ongoing professional development based on collaboration, team development, and co-teaching.

### School Culture

- Examine the school's physical structure to determine locations conducive to planning, supporting, and implementing inclusion at each grade level.
- Create a schedule that promotes consistent and common planning time for ongoing communication and dialogue.
- Develop and implement approaches and procedures that promote a professional learning community (collaboration, consensus, agreeing to disagree respectfully).

- Purposefully build a classroom and school climate that is warm and welcoming for children and staff and fosters active, engaged learning.

## MAP CURRENT SERVICE DELIVERY

Teams examine the existing way services are provided, human resources are used, and where students receive which services. This process requires that school teams map out current service delivery and human resource distribution in an effort to meet the range of student needs. This involves creating a visual representation of the classrooms, special education service provision, general education classrooms, and where students receive their related services. An essential part of creating service maps is to indicate which staff pull students from which classrooms, which students learn in self-contained spaces, and which paraprofessionals are used where—a complete picture of how and where all staff at the school work.

***Examples.*** Figure 6.1 provides an example of this kind of visual map of the service delivery model before inclusive school reform. The rectangles around the edge represent the general education classrooms. The ovals in the middle labeled "Resource" represent resource special education teachers who work with students with disabilities in many classrooms (as indicated by the lines) through a pullout model. The circles labeled Self-Contained are a multi-aged group of students with disabilities who spend the entire day together and apart from their general education peers. There is one oval marked Inclusion 20+10. This represents what was previously called an inclusive classroom. This room had about 20 general education students with an additional 10 students with disabilities. This old service delivery plan segregated students with intense needs into certain classrooms while other classrooms lacked students with disabilities and additional adult support. Some students were excluded and removed from the general education curriculum, instruction, and social interaction with their general education peers for part or all of each school day.

We see visual mapping of services as a key way to understand the patterns of who gets which kinds of services and where these services happen. Visual mapping of services can also allow leaders and teams to see racial and socioeconomic patterns of student composition in classes and services (see Figure 6.2).

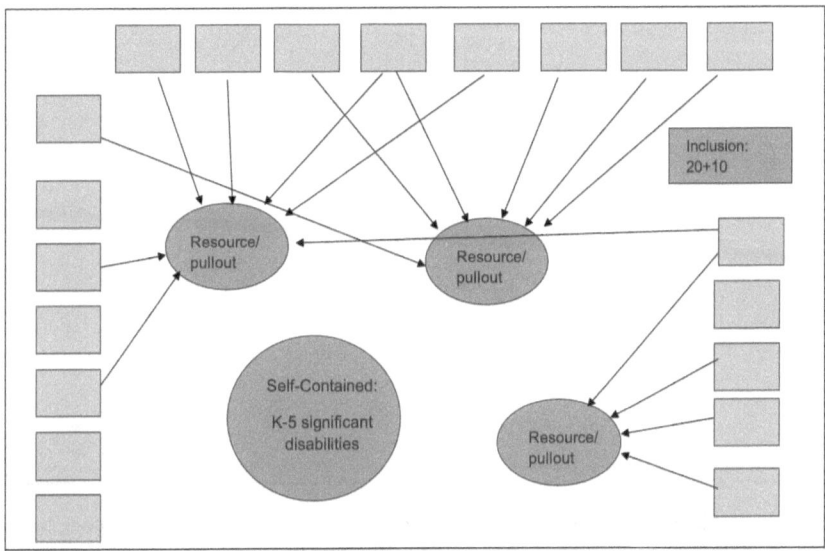

Figure 6.1. Special education service delivery prior to inclusive restructuring. *Note: Rectangles = elementary general education classrooms K–5. Circles/ovals = special education teachers. Resource = special education teachers who pull students from their general education classroom. Inclusion 20+10 = a classroom where a general education teacher is team teaching with a special education teacher where there are 20 general education students and 10 special education students. Self-contained: K–5 significant disabilities = a special education classroom where all students who have significant disabilities receive their instruction and spend the majority of their school day.*

Creating service maps and identifying the race, social class, gender, and language of students who are being pulled out of classrooms and the students who remain in the classroom visually shows the ways that segregating students typically marginalizes students of color, linguistically diverse students, low-income students, and privileges White and middle-class students. These maps then allow leaders and school teams to have conversations about these inequitable patterns. For example, Figure 6.2 shows one classroom of elementary students, with the circles on the bottom representing students and the individual students who were pulled out before inclusive reform.

While this process for inclusive school reform was originally designed for inclusion of students with disabilities, we have used the same process to create more inclusive services for students who are culturally and linguistically diverse. In those cases, the teachers of and service providers for students who were ELLs were represented on the service maps instead of special education teachers (see Figure 6.3).

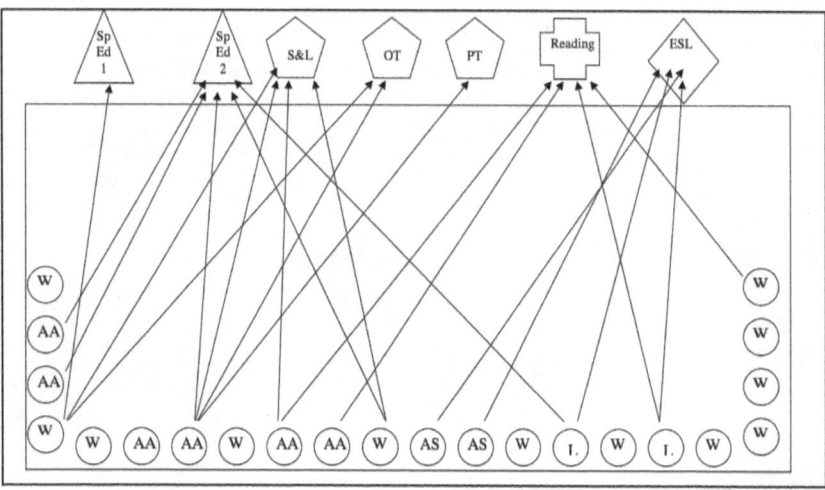

Figure 6.2. Elementary classroom—Disrupted by the pullout services provided. Note: Shapes on top represent staff members and their corresponding pullout program: Sp Ed = special ed. teacher. S&L = speech & language therapist. OT = occupational therapist. PT = physical therapist. Reading = Title I reading teacher. ESL = English as a Second Language teacher. Circles on the sides and bottom represent the students; labeled by race: AA = African American, AS = Asian, L = Latino, W = White.

## REALIGN SCHOOL AND STAFFING STRUCTURE BASED ON THAT BOLD VISION

This step involves rethinking structures and the use of staff to create teams of professionals to serve all students inclusively; in other words, the goal is to create a new service delivery map that moves the school toward the bold vision laid out in the first step. The staff develops a new inclusive service delivery plan by redeploying staff to create balanced and heterogeneous classrooms where all students are included. An essential component of this step is placing students in classrooms using the school's actual proportion of students with special education needs or other needs (like ELL) as a guide as previously defined.

*Example.* Figure 6.4 provides an example of inclusive service delivery where teachers and administrators reconfigured the current use of staff (Figure 6.1) to form teams of specialists and general education teachers to create inclusive teams that collaboratively planned and delivered instruction to heterogeneous student groups (seen in Figure 6.4). In this example the school chose to pair special education teachers as part of inclusive teams with

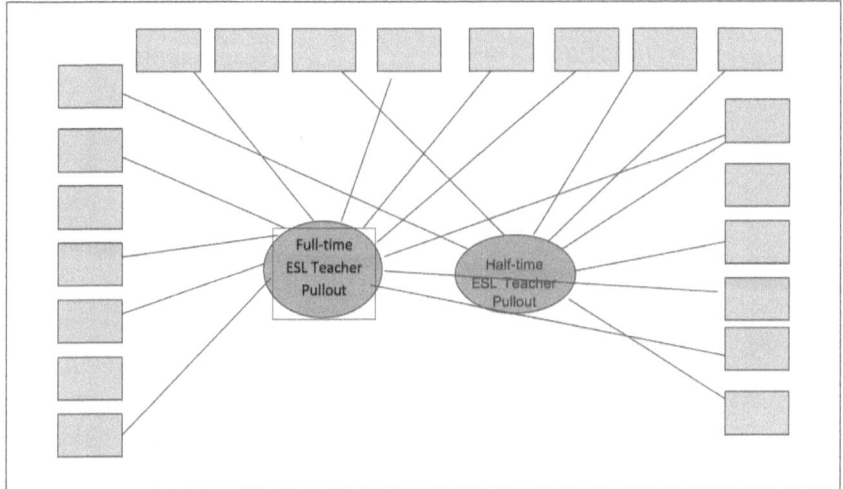

Figure 6.3. ELL service delivery prior to inclusive restructuring. *Note: Rectangles = elementary general education classrooms. Ovals = ESL teachers. Pullout = ESL teacher taking ELL students to an ESL resource room to provide instruction. Lines = the classrooms from which ESL teachers pull students for the ESL program.*

two to three general education classrooms and teachers. This was not about dumping students with needs into a particular classroom, it was about creating heterogeneous spaces. This necessitated focusing each year on creating heterogeneous classrooms that balanced students' needs across all rooms or sections and kept the actual student population proportions front and center. "Actual proportions" means that if 13% of the students at the school have disabilities, then the student placement process mirrors that density of students with disabilities in each classroom. Classrooms should not be created such that students with disabilities (and thus with a need for additional support) are highly concentrated in some spaces and not in others. Part of creating classes at any level is to not segregate students with special education needs into one room or section. Using actual proportions as a guide, it is important to strive for balanced and heterogeneous classes that mix abilities, achievement, behavior, and other learning parameters.

Figure 6.5 provides an example of a redesigned ESL program based on the original (Figure 6.3). About 16% of the students were in the ESL program, and across the school there were 12 languages other than English spoken at home. When it made sense based on the children, this school tried to pair students who spoke the same home language in the same class to not isolate students. This school worked to have ESL teachers co-plan and co-deliver instruction with one to two teachers per grade level (Figure 6.5). A principal involved in this service delivery redesign said, "Mapping the service delivery

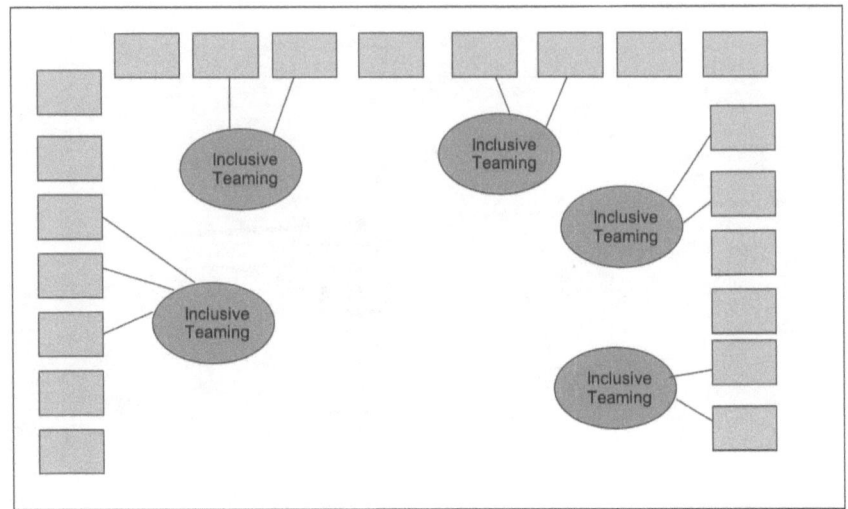

Figure 6.4. Inclusive service delivery for students with disabilities. *Note: Rectangles = elementary general education classrooms. Circles/ovals = special education teachers. Inclusive teaming = a special education teacher teaming with two to three regular education teachers to meet the range of student needs within the classroom. Each team has one paraprofessional assigned as well.*

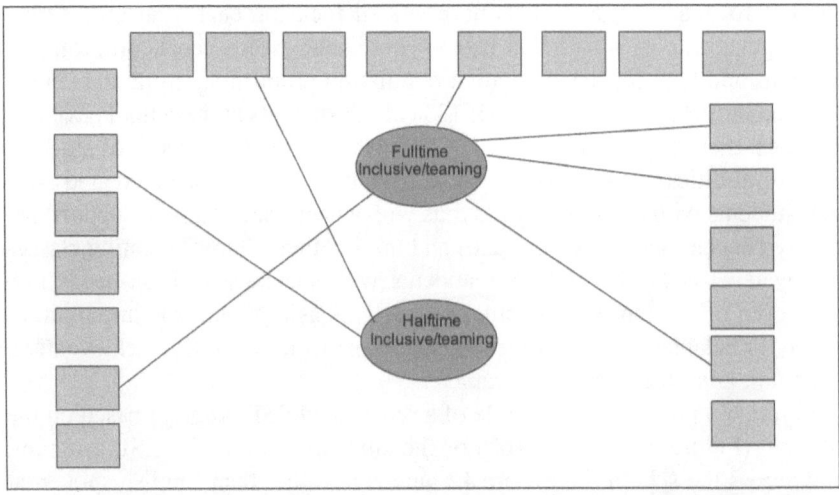

Figure 6.5. Inclusive service delivery for ESL program. *Note: Rectangles = elementary general education classrooms. Ovals = ESL teachers. Inclusive/teaming = an ENL teacher teaming with regular education teachers to meet the range of student need within the classroom.*

gave our whole team the ability to see and understand how we serve our students with disabilities. That led to our team creating a more inclusive model built on collaboration." A teacher involved in this stated, "This was hard work, but because we created the more inclusive model together, staff felt ownership."

## BUILD INSTRUCTIONAL TEAMS TO TRANSFORM CLASSROOM PRACTICE

Rethinking staff involves creating teams of general education teachers, specialists (i.e., special education teachers, ELL teachers, etc.), and paraprofessionals to serve all students inclusively. In Figures 6.1 and 6.4, the special education teacher who was formerly a teacher in a self-contained classroom (Figure 6.1) is now part of a teaching team and co-plans and co-delivers instruction with two general education teachers (Figure 6.4) and a paraprofessional.

Culturally responsive and socially just leaders develop instructional teams of specialists and generalists. These teams are the ones who provide services, teach, and carry out the plan described in the previous section. Developing teams takes on different forms, but at its core involves bringing together professionals who will share a responsibility to work together to inclusively meet the needs of the range of learners under their joint care. This requires revising the roles many professionals previously played in their schools and building trust between those members. It is essential that in addition to developing teams the leader supports those teams and gives them common planning time.

It is important when building instructional teams that leaders work to transform the daily classroom practices supported by teaching teams. This involves creating and carrying out a professional development (PD) plan for teachers, paraprofessionals, and administrators. We recommend that schools consider topics such as collaboration, team or co-teaching, differentiated instruction, working with challenging behavior, inquiry-based instruction, and ELL methods, among others. In our experience, schools that have become more inclusive through this process have spent significant PD time and energy on collaboration, teaching teams, and differentiation. A component of transforming classroom practices and the PD required to do that involves school leaders setting expectations and providing feedback to their staff.

*Example.* After mapping out the current service delivery model and realigning school and staffing structures based on the school's vision, school leaders must work to build their instructional teams to transform classroom practice. For example, in a school that shifted from mainly providing services in self-contained classrooms and minimal push-in services (similar to Figure 6.1) to an inclusive service delivery model similar to that of Figure 6.4, the leaders focused on these three elements to build instructional teams and transform classroom practice through common planning time, clear expectations and feedback, and prioritization of opportunities for PD concerning related goals for inclusive practices.

The school leaders worked with teachers to shift to a delivery model similar to what is shown in Figure 6.4. As discussed earlier, realigning the staffing structure to provide more inclusive services permits the creation of more heterogeneous spaces for students. When realigning school and staff structures, special education teachers were reassigned from their previous schedules (split between grade levels and service delivery models) to only teaching in general education rooms and only in one grade level or one content area. This change allowed special education teachers to go from working with multiple grade levels and in multiple settings (e.g., both in the general education classroom and in self-contained classrooms) to providing services in the general education classroom for only one grade level. This change in schedule and role permitted specialists to have a main role in the general education classrooms and consistently have a common planning time with the team (general education teachers and other specialists).

As the specialists were working solely with one grade level, they were now regularly free during that grade level's common planning time. A special education teacher reflected on this: "Planning together, even once a week, made a huge difference in our ability to meet students' needs." Previously specialists were not consistently available for common planning as they were split among grade levels and classrooms. Figure 6.6 gives an example of two special education teachers' schedules who provided services in the general education classrooms for two content areas. As depicted in Figure 6.6, the special education teachers were able to specialize in one content area while the grade level's planning time was built into the specialists' schedule. When the expectation is for instructional teams to provide joint care by providing services in general education, the space and support must be provided. Having built-in planning time was essential for the instructional team to co-plan and co-deliver instruction. The school worked to have special education teachers specialize in content areas in addition to solely working on one grade level. The planning time was utilized for co-planning among the co-teaching team and meeting with larger instructional teams (e.g., instructional coaches, other content teachers, and grade level teachers). The increased amount of shared time among the instructional team also provided time to foster relationships and grow trust among general education teachers, specialists, and paraprofessionals.

Shifting teachers' roles (general education teachers, specialists, and paraprofessionals) entailed changes in expectations. As such, those expectations were clearly communicated and developed with goals for the teams' co-planning and co-delivery of instruction. Accordingly the school leaders and the instructional team developed goal areas together that were aligned with the new role expectations, co-teaching, and the school's overall commitments to inclusive services. This PD and learning included both informal and formal opportunities such as instructional coaching, focused grade-level collaboration, and school-wide PD sessions. A consistent focus on the school's commitment (versus one-off PD) to inclusive services and alignment to the related goals in PD resulted in growing trust among educators as well as strengthened inclusive practices.

## CONCLUSION

As socially just leaders work to take on inclusive schooling, they must be prepared to stand firm in their vision and commitments in the face of resistance and challenges. There has been and will always be resistance to service delivery changes. Leadership is needed to establish and maintain direction, engage staff and families, and annually improve service delivery to improve inclusivity. We have seen a movement away from inclusive services with the competing demands of policies such as Race to the Top (RTTT) and with challenges posed by the COVID–19 pandemic. New policies and mechanisms have brought hesitation and resistance from educators. It is in these moments that leaders must hold firm to their commitments, maintain inclusive service deliveries, and lean on the collaboration of instructional teams.

| 7th Grade Math Special Education Teacher | | | 7th Grade ELA Special Education Teacher | | |
|---|---|---|---|---|---|
| Period 1 | 7 Math | General Education Cohort A | Period 1 | 7 ELA | General Education Cohort D |
| Period 2 | 7 Math | General Education Cohort B | Period 2 | 7 ELA | General Education Cohort C |
| Period 3 | 7th Grade Planning Period | | Period 3 | 7th Grade Planning Period | |
| Period 4 | 7 Math | General Education Cohort C | Period 4 | 7 ELA | General Education Cohort B |
| Period 5 | 7 Math | General Education Cohort D | Period 5 | 7 ELA | General Education Cohort A |

**Figure 6.6.** Special education teacher schedule for inclusive service delivery model.

In this chapter we have outlined four key steps that will help socially just leaders create and engage in inclusive services.[16] A central element of such leadership for those concerned with creating socially just schools is grounding that leadership in the belief that it is their job and responsibility to create just and more-equitable schools.

We know segregated, self-contained services for students receiving special education and ELL services are less effective and in opposition to just and equitable schooling. This chapter has brought to light the ways in which socially just leaders *can* and *should*, with the support and collaboration of their teams, create and maintain inclusive services.

## REFLECTIVE QUESTIONS

- In what ways does your school provide inclusive services to students with disabilities and ELLs? In what ways does it not?
- What do you think are impediments in the classroom and school system that hinder inclusivity?
- What does your special education service delivery look like? ENL? Create a visual of your services.
- As a school leader, what is your role in addressing issues of inclusivity? What is your own bold vision for inclusive service delivery?

## NOTES

1. National Center for Education Statistics, 2019.
2. U.S. Department of Education, 2020.
3. U.S. Department of Education, 2020; Connor, Ferri, & Annamma, 2016.
4. Frattura & Capper, 2007.
5. Ruiz-de-Velasco & Fix, 2000.
6. Thomas & Collier, 2012.
7. Cosier, Causton-Theoharis, & Theoharis, 2013; Krämer, Möller, & Zimmermann, 2021.
8. Frattura & Capper, 2007; Radd, Generett, Gooden, & Theoharis, 2021; Theoharis, 2007; Theoharis & Scanlan, 2020.
9. Collier & Thomas, 2012.
10. Dove & Honigsfeld, 2010; Honigsfeld, Dove, Cohan, & Goldman, 2021; Maxwell, 2013; Theoharis & O'Toole, 2011; Thomas & Collier, 2012.
11. Kunc, 1992, pp. 38–39.
12. Causton-Theoharis & Theoharis, 2008, p. 45.
13. Kozleski, Artiles, & Waitoller, 2014.
14. Theoharis, Causton, Woodfield, & Scribner, 2020.

15. Causton & Theoharis, 2014, p. 145.
16. Theoharis, Causton, Woodfield, & Scribner, 2020.

## REFERENCES

Causton, J., & Theoharis, G. (2014). *The principal's handbook for leading inclusive schools*. Bookes Publishing.
Causton-Theoharis, J., & Theoharis, G. (2008). Creating inclusive schools for all students. *School Administrator*, 24–30.
Collier, V. P., & Thomas, W. P. (2012). What really works for English language learners: Research based practices for principals. In G. Theoharis & J. Brooks (Eds.), *What every principal needs to know: Instructional leadership for equitable & excellent schools.* (pp. 155–173). Teachers College Press.
Connor, D., Ferri, B., & Annamma, S. (2016). *Discrit: Disability studies and critical race theory in education*. Teachers College Press.
Cosier, M., Causton-Theoharis, J., & Theoharis, G. (2013). Does access matter? Time in general education and achievement for students with disabilities. *Remedial and Special Education, 34*(6), 323–332.
Dove, M., & Honigsfeld, A. (2010). ESL co-teaching and collaboration: Opportunities to develop teacher leadership and enhance student learning. *TESOL Journal*.
Frattura, E., & Capper, C. A. (2007). *Leading for social justice: Transforming schools for all learners*. Corwin Press.
Honigsfeld, A., Dove, M. G., Cohan, A. F., & Goldman, C. M. (2021). *From equity insights to action: Critical strategies for teaching multilingual learners*. Corwin Press.
Individuals with Disabilities Education Improvement Act of 2004, 20 U.S.C. 1401 et seq. (2004). (Reauthorization of the Individuals with Disabilities Education Act of 1990).
Kozleski, E. B., Artiles, A., & Waitoller, F. (2014). Translating inclusive education: Equity concerns. *The handbook of special education*, 231–249.
Krämer, S., Möller, J., & Zimmermann, F. (2021). Inclusive education of students with general learning difficulties: A meta-analysis. *Review of Educational Research, 91*(3): 432–478. https://doi.org.10.3102/0034654321998072
Kunc, N. (1992). The need to belong: Rediscovering Maslow's hierarchy of needs. In R. A. Villa, J. S. Thousand, W. Stainback, & S. Stainback (Eds.), *Restructuring for caring and effective education: An administrative guide to creating heterogeneous schools* (pp. 25–39). Paul H. Brookes Publishing.
Maxwell, L. (2013). Minn. superintendent pioneered ELL reforms. *Ed Week*, January 29, 2013. https://www.edweek.org/leaders/2013/minn-superintendent-pioneered-ell-reforms/00000173-3922-df16-ab7f-7967509a0003
National Center for Educational Statistics (2019). Table 204.50: Children 3 to 21 years old served under Individuals with Disabilities Education Act (IDEA), Part B, by age group and sex, race/ethnicity, and type of disability: 2017–18. Retrieved

online September 29, 2019 from https://nces.ed.gov/programs/digest/d18/tables/dt18_204.50.asp

Radd, S., Generett, G. G., Gooden, M. A., & Theoharis, G. (2021). *Five practices for leading equity-focused school leadership.* ASCD.

Ruiz-de-Velasco, J., & Fix, M. (2000). *Overlooked & underserved: Immigrant students in U.S. secondary schools.* Washington, DC: Urban Institute.

Theoharis, G., Causton, J., Woodfield, C., & Scribner, S. (2020). Leading inclusive schools for students with disabilities. In G. Theoharis & M. Scanlan (Eds.), *Inclusive leadership for increasingly diverse schools.* Routledge.

Theoharis, G., & O'Toole, J. (2011). Leading inclusive ELL: Social justice leadership for English language learners. *Educational Administration Quarterly, 47*(4), 646–688.

Theoharis, G., & Scanlan, M. (Eds.). (2020). *Leadership for increasingly diverse schools.* Routledge.

United States Department of Education (2020). *41st annual report to Congress on the implementation of the Individuals with Disabilities Education Act, 2020: Resource Document.* Washington, DC, pp. 38–161.

*Chapter 7*

# Tribe–School District Relationships for Policy Change toward Social Justice

Mona Halcomb, Washington Office of Superintendent of Public Instruction

### KEY TAKEAWAYS

- Native Americans have been disenfranchised by American schools throughout history and it still continues today.
- Oregon was the first state in the nation to codify into law a government-to-government relationship between the nine federally recognized tribes and the state in 1975. Tribal education directors meet each quarter to share best practices and priorities.
- The Oregon Department of Education's commitment to Native American students has resulted in an unprecedented increase in the graduation rate for these students, growing 11% in the past five years.
- Oregon's American Indian/Alaska Native State Plan focuses on learners, educators, schools and districts, community voice, and the Oregon Department of Education's building of internal systems and processes to support equity initiatives.
- One-third of Oregon tribally enrolled students missed 10% or more school days in 2011–2012. Tribal Attendance Promising Practices helped improve attendance by using intentional strategies.
- The nine federally recognized tribes in Oregon advocated for changes in the teacher certification process for their Master Teacher in Language

License and found alternative ways to allow heritage language teachers into the classroom. They included native languages in the Oregon State Seal of Biliteracy as well.

The concrete steps felt cold as I sat next to my mom. She was wearing pedal pushers and a brown-and-white checkered shirt tied in the front. I wondered if she could hear my knees knocking as I tried to find the words to beg her not to send me to school. My five-year-old mind failed to come up with anything to let her know how uncomfortable I was there.

My mother attended the Chemawa Indian Boarding School in Salem, Oregon. Like many boarding school survivors, she will *not* discuss her boarding school story with her family. There are many books and articles on these overcrowded, underfunded institutions riddled with all sorts of abuse.[1] In researching boarding schools, I found another source of articles worth exploring later, academic articles noting a correlation between the poor health of Native American children and the role economics and poverty plays in their health outcomes.[2] The articles fail to mention that poverty is due to treaties not upheld with the Native Americans.

I say I am a product of boarding schools as both my mother and father attended Indian boarding schools. The infamous phrase of Richard Pratt "Kill the Indian, save the man" is well documented. The forced break–up of families, the forced abandonment of community, language, and spiritual practices, left many soul wounds impacting Indian families and communities for generations.[3] Not being allowed to speak their native language took away their ability to even articulate the abuse, and students could no longer communicate in their heritage language with their families when they returned home. I heard children were punished when they spoke their native language at boarding school. What I did not know was that older children were forced to punish the younger students for speaking their native language. My father told me having to punish younger children was one of the most painful memories he had of being kidnapped and taken to boarding school. He had to beat younger boys or face getting beat himself. Native Americans were thought to be less than human and were treated as such in society, and boarding schools reflected this perspective. An accurate description of this can be summed up in "Indians were the first prisoners of war."[4] I believe this led to the lateral violence Indian people inflict on one another today.

As you can imagine, even if my five-year-old mind could have come up with an argument for not sending me to school, since my mother survived boarding school, I doubt I could have been convincing. My school days were full of fear and ridicule, and I was the embodiment of an At Promise youth. I came from a single parent household and lived in poverty, and academics were second to caring for my younger siblings. What was etched into my mind was my high school counselor telling me, "Go join the military or work in a factory because that is *all* you'll ever be capable of."

There were a few gifted educators. One I remember reached out to me because I was always getting suspended for smoking in the girls room. He'd called me into his office, slammed the door, and said, "Darn it, if you want a cigarette, come in here, shut the door, and smoke! Just don't get caught and sent home." When I found myself pregnant, he helped me go to school in a teen mother program and graduate with my class. These classes taught the basics of being a new mother. Physical education class was focused on nutrition for newborns and how to bathe an infant and change diapers. When I went into labor, he even drove me to the hospital. I owe graduating from high school to his dedication and commitment to getting me through a system not built for me.

My daughter did not have any better experiences in school. When she was in sixth grade her teacher stood over her desk and in front of the whole class shouted, "What is wrong with you? I have had retards learn math faster than you!" Despite my going to school and having a meeting with the teacher and principal to ask for an apology, nothing happened. In fact, I believe the teacher became even more verbally abusive and emboldened to be demeaning to my daughter. She is proud of going to Northwest Indian College and getting a B in algebra.

My grandson experienced too many negative examples in school to list or choose just one. In talking with him, we decided one of the more painful times was when a counselor told him, "You'll never keep a job, even if it's flipping hamburgers!" This statement stings him even today at thirty years old. When I asked about a positive example of school, he thought for a long time and remembered his fourth-grade teacher Mrs. Scott. She was patient and kind. She did not immediately send kids to the principal and "look for what you were doing wrong." Mrs. Scott would take the time to work through difficult circumstances and would problem solve rather than pass you off as a problem to someone else.

My granddaughter is gifted. She cried because she realized she'd run out of math classes before she graduated from high school. Since the time she could talk she has said she wanted to be a pediatrician or veterinarian. Her dream was ripped from her with one statement from her counselor. She was told, "Why do you want to put all that pressure on yourself? Why don't you just be a nurse's aide to see if you like it and can handle the medical field?" That counselor projected her own limited thinking onto my gifted granddaughter. When I tried to convince her that her counselor didn't know her and that she was smart and could handle medical school, she responded with "Oh, Nana, you have to say that because you love me." My granddaughter moved during her senior year and this affected her academic progress. She was getting far behind, but she was able to turn things around with a supportive teacher who helped her graduate. Today I am proud of her because she has always loved animals and she has become a veterinary technician. She has been promoted and is considering continuing her education in veterinary science.

My great-granddaughter is in fourth grade. When she was in kindergarten, an older student would continually bully her. Her family spoke with the school several times. On the bus the older student punctured her with a pencil. It is unfortunate that too many brown and poor students are not given positive environments that encourage safe learning places. She loves math and when we took her to a marine museum, she really enjoyed looking in a microscope and touching aquatic life. It is too early to tell what her education experience will be like. One of the reasons I continue working is hoping to influence positive change in the educational experience of all students especially Native American and Alaska Native students.

Some educators might believe it is the make-up of a school's demographics, the instructional staff, curriculum, or funding that makes a difference in the experience of students. In the stories of my five generations, the schools ranged from almost all American Indian and Alaska Native students, to less than 1%. And still there was a common thread of harm. Not only were low expectations evident, there was an outright effort to discourage following one's dreams.

In my family's education there were bright lights, people who went above and beyond their job to make a difference. Therein is the problem. It was the efforts of a few good people and not a systematic approach. Often when positive efforts are based on individuals, those efforts shift or stop once the person leaves. Real change is only possible when efforts transcend personal commitments and become embedded in the strategic plans and mission statements of educational systems.

In five generations' experiences one would hope assimilation, abuse, low academic expectations, bullying, humiliation, and discouragement would not continue in any school system. Unfortunately, looking at my story of five generations, this is not the case. Many institutions and educators say their goal is "serving the underserved, centering equity, and providing well-rounded high-quality education to all students." In case one thinks these experiences are unique to my family, I encourage them to read "Meriam Report: The Problem of Indian Administration";[5] "Indian Education: A National Tragedy—A National Challenge (Kennedy Report)";[6] and "2014 Native Youth Report."[7] These reports show the deplorable education provided Native American Youth has not changed in 86 years. No matter how often we hear that institutions are committed to change, actions speak louder than words. Many educators are surprised when I ask them their thoughts about "well-rounded education" and then tell them this term was mentioned in the

1928 Meriam Report and that Native American communities are still waiting to see this promise fulfilled.

But even when schools want to change (and that is sometimes a rash assumption), administrators can be ineffective because of being more invested in protecting their job instead of meeting community and student needs.[8] Or worse than not caring[9] or protecting your job is the exhaustion and burnout some teachers experience when they feel like there is no other way to deal with the stress, demands, or conditions students face outside their classrooms. I do not blame leaders for wanting to protect their job or burning out. Looking at the research on the intersectionality of race and gender regarding leadership, these are at the top.[10] The challenges of social norms for gender and ethnic roles influence how diverse leaders are seen and evaluated.[11]

How can we positively affect the 105,120 hours students should be in school and bring educational opportunities more in line with the beautifully crafted mission statements institutions painstakingly write? This chapter will look at some of the positive strategies Oregon has taken to change the educational landscape for American Indian and Alaska Native youth.

## GOVERNMENT-TO-GOVERNMENT

Oregon was the first state in the nation to codify into law a government-to-government relationship between the nine federally recognized tribes in Oregon and the state in 1975. The Legislative Commission on Indian Services was created per ORS 172.100.[12] The Legislative Commission on Indian Services is comprised of two Oregon Senators, Two Oregon House Representatives, tribal chairs from all nine federally recognized tribes in Oregon, and one member-at-large on behalf of the urban Native voice.

It is important to understand the creation of the Legislative Commission on Indian Services did not provide tribal sovereignty; rather, this recognized inherent tribal sovereignty predating the existence of the United States and the State of Oregon. Article VI of the United States Constitution states,

> This Constitution, and the Laws of the United States which shall be made in Pursuance thereof; and all Treaties made, or which shall be made, under the Authority of the United States, shall be the supreme Law of the Land; and the Judges in every State shall be bound thereby, any Thing in the Constitution or Laws of any State to the Contrary notwithstanding.[13]

Tribal governments self-govern, with the right to form their own government, to make and enforce their own laws, and to determine their citizenship criteria. There are only two things beyond tribal governments' jurisdiction:

minting money and declaring war.[14] Due to the extensive jurisdiction of tribal governments, the government-to-government format is to have clusters meet and focus on certain aspects. Every quarter the tribal education directors of all nine federally recognized tribes meet with the director of education, director of the early learning division, the director of the Higher Education Coordinating Commission, the director of the Youth Development Division, the director of the Teacher Standards and Practices Commission, and the governor's chief policy advisor. The Tribal Education Cluster has one day when the tribal education directors meet and share best practices and priorities. The next day all state agency directors inform the tribes of any upcoming efforts that will impact American Indian and Alaska Native youth. Working together the tribes and state agencies collaborate with the intent of serving American Indian and Alaska Native youth in Oregon. Let's look at a few of the structures and initiatives implemented by Oregon that have been successful in Oregon in recent years.

## OFFICE OF INDIAN EDUCATION

Before November 2013 the Oregon Department of Education had a .10 full-time equivalent (FTE) position dedicated to Indian education. The nine federally recognized tribes in Oregon advocated for more of a commitment to serving American Indian and Alaska Native students. The Oregon Department of Education hired a full-time Indian education specialist. Originally this position was placed in the Office of Diversity, Equity, and Inclusion. However the nine federally recognized tribes advocated that since the tribes and the state had a government-to-government relationship, the Indian education specialist should report directly to the deputy superintendent of public instruction. The Oregon Department of Education then moved the Indian education specialist to the director's office. As a result of the American Indian/Alaska Native State Plan revision, in 2016 the Oregon Department of Education hired another Indian education specialist to help implement the plan and support the needs of American Indian and Alaska Native students and youth in Oregon. In 2019 our office became officially the Office of Indian Education. At the time of writing, the Office of Indian Education has four full-time staff and two graduate interns dedicated to serving students.

The Oregon Department of Education's investment has seen results because of their commitment as evidenced by an unprecedented increase in the graduation rate for American Indian and Alaska Native students, growing 11% in the past five years.

## AMERICAN INDIAN/ALASKA NATIVE ADVISORY COMMITTEE

Having a framework prevents efforts from only being propelled by individual passions rather than a structure. The history of the Office of Indian Education is a perfect example. Before late 2013, the Oregon Department of Education had as noted a .10 FTE position dedicated to Native American education. The Tribal Education Cluster advocated for a full-time position. The department listened and hired a full-time employee. Oregon's Native American Education Plan was twenty years old and not well known or implemented at the time.

The Oregon Department of Education created an American Indian/Alaska Native Advisory Committee to update the American Indian/Alaska Native Education State Plan. It is important to understand that the American Indian/Alaska Native Advisory Committee advises the Office of Indian Education, and the Tribal Education Cluster approves the state plan and other efforts provided by our office. After nine months, the 2015 Native American State Education Plan was created.[15] The new plan establishes eleven goals.

- Increase graduation rates for American Indian and Alaska Native students.
- Increase college or career readiness of American Indian and Alaska Native students.
- Increase American Indian and Alaska Native attendance.
- Increase the number of American Indian and Alaska Native teachers and administrators.
- Provide culturally responsive professional development.
- Encourage graduates of Oregon teacher preparatory schools to stay in Oregon.
- Develop legislative language of accurate tribal history and shared history curriculum.
- Hold community conversations with tribal communities and educational stakeholders.
- Use data justice to reduce erasure of American Indian and Alaska Native youth.
- Monitor accountability of implementation of plan by reporting to the State Board of Education and produce an annual report.
- Continue to build internal agency capacity.

The American Indian/Alaska Native State Plan was well designed since it focused on learners, educators, schools and districts, community voice, and the Oregon Department of Education's internal systems and processes supporting equity initiatives. The American Indian/Alaska Native Education

State Plan was approved by the Oregon State Board of Education in 2014 and updated in 2016. In addition, the Office of Indian Education provided professional development to school administrators and leaders on how to implement the American Indian/Alaska Native Education State Plan. We gave presentations at state and national events for organizations such as the Coalition of Oregon School Administrators, Oregon School Boards Association, Oregon Education Association, Oregon Indian Education Association, National Indian Education Association, and Affiliated Tribes of Northwest Indians. Let's take a closer look at some of the goals of this plan.

## TRIBAL ATTENDANCE PROMISING PRACTICES

A 2014 report, "The Condition of Education for Members of Oregon's Indian Tribes,"[16] revealed one-third of Oregon tribally enrolled students missed 10% or more school days in 2011–2012. Ten percent or more is considered chronic absenteeism. The report found 195 of their peers were chronically absent. The Tribal Education Cluster advocated for funds to address chronic absenteeism, and the Oregon Legislature funded the Tribal Attendance Pilot Project, which four successful years later was named Tribal Attendance Promising Practices. I believe the strength of Tribal Attendance Promising Practices is built into the structure of the grant.

- The nine federally recognized tribes in Oregon select which school district they would like to partner with.
- The tribe and the school district co-create a job description for a family advocate.
- The tribe approves of the applicant pool, and the school district hires and supervises the family advocate.
- The tribe, school district, and family advocate create strategies to increase attendance.
- Of the nine school districts and seventeen schools in Tribal Attendance Promising Practices, each site has strategies unique to its district and population.
- The Oregon Department of Education creates messaging campaigns on the importance of school attendance.
- The Oregon Department of Education provides technical support and training for the family advocates and other educational partners.
- The Oregon Department of Education reports on the effectiveness of Tribal Attendance Promising Practices and shares best practices.

## LANGUAGE AND THE TEACHER CERTIFICATION PROCESS

The nine federally recognized tribes in Oregon advocated for changes in the teacher certification process for their Master Teacher in Language License knowing that many of the remaining Native teachers were elders and not about to go back to school for a traditional teacher's license. The Teacher Standards and Practices Commission understood this and worked with the tribes to find alternative ways to allow heritage language teachers into the classroom. The tribes now write a letter certifying someone is qualified to teach their languages, and that person is awarded certification allowing them to teach the heritage language in Oregon's K–12 schools. Several colleges offer heritage languages too.

## THE OFFICE OF INDIAN EDUCATION

The Oregon School Board created the Oregon State Seal of Biliteracy. This recognizes and values the native languages students speak. As such, a student literate in reading, writing, listening, and speaking in one or more world languages in addition to English is eligible to earn the seal. The biliteracy seal was awarded to American Indian students speaking Chinuk Wawa, Nez Perce, and Umatilla. The Oregon State Seal of Biliteracy was the first in the nation to collaborate with post-secondary institutions. Research confirms you can't separate language and culture.[17] And tribal sovereignty and self-determination recognize that a healthy democracy should not be monolithic.[18]

## CONCLUSION

I have seen the ways in which American schools have and continue to be inhospitable to Native American students. I credit a caring teacher with helping me finish school and get me where I am today so that I can serve as a social justice leader in my community. In my work as an Indian education specialist with the Oregon Department of Education's Office of Indian Education, I have participated in the implementation of numerous policies and practices that strive to improve opportunities and expand access for Native American students in the state. I am hopeful that future generations of Native Americans in the state of Oregon will experience a more welcoming and culturally responsive environment in school and that these reforms will expand to other states across the country. We are the native people of the

United States and deserve to have access to the same quality of education as others. In sharing my story, I hope to inform the leadership of schools and districts so that the needs of Native American students are central.

## REFLECTIVE QUESTIONS

- How do you support Native American students in your school or district?
- How might policies in your area better support the needs of Native students?
- Are there policies and practices in place that serve to disenfranchise Native students? How might they be adapted to be more affirming?
- How do you incorporate the lessons of Native American history and culture in your school environment for all students?
- How can we use the personal narratives of disenfranchised groups to inform our practices as school and district leaders?

## NOTES

1. Meriam report: The problem of Indian administration (1928). https://narf.org/nill/resources/meriam.html

2. Townsend, J. G. (1938). Disease and the Indian. *Scientific Monthly, 47*(6), 479–495. https://www.jstor.org/stable/1662

3. Little, B. (2018). Government boarding schools once separated Native American children from families. https://www.history.com/news/government-boarding-schools-separated-native-american-children-families

4. Chavers, D. (1974). Indian education: Failure for the future? *American Indian Law Review, 2*(1), 61–84.

5. Meriam report: The problem of Indian administration (1928).

6. U.S. Senate Committee on Labor and Public Welfare. (1969). Indian education: A national tragedy—A national challenge (Kennedy report). https://collegefund.org/research/indian-education-a-national-tragedy-a-national-challenge-kennedy-report-1969/

7. Executive Office of the President. (2014). 2014 Native youth report. https://obamawhitehouse.archives.gov/sites/default/files/docs/20141129nativeyouthreport_final.pdf

8. Stovall, D. (2004). School leader as negotiator: Critical race theory, praxis, and the creation of productive space. *Multicultural Education, 12*(2), 8–12.

9. Haberman, M. (2005). Teacher burnout in Black and White. *New Educator, 1*(3), 153–175. https://doi.org.10.1080/15476880590966303

10. Chin, J. L. (2013). Diversity leadership: Influence of ethnicity, gender, and minority status. *Open Journal of Leadership, 2*(1), 1.

11. Chin, J. L., 2013.
12. Oregon State Legislature. https://www.oregonlegislature.gov/cis/Pages/minutesAgendas.aspx
13. U.S. Constitution.
14. U.S. Department of the Interior. (2022). Indian affairs. www.bia.gov.
15. Oregon American Indian/Alaska Native Education State Plan 2015. (2015).
16. The condition of education for members of Oregon's Indian tribes. (2014). www.betteroregon.org
17. Yazzie, E. P. (2003). Missionaries and American Indian languages.
18. Lomawaima, K. T., & McCarty, T. L. (2002). When tribal sovereignty challenges democracy: American Indian education and the democratic ideal. *American Educational Research Journal, 39*(2), 279–305. https://doi.org/10.3102/00028312039002279

## REFERENCES

Chavers, D. (1974). Indian education: Failure for the future? *American Indian Law Review, 2*(1), 61–84.

Chin, J. L. (2013). Diversity leadership: Influence of ethnicity, gender, and minority status. *Open Journal of Leadership, 2*(1), 1.

Condition of Education for Members of Oregon's Indian Tribes. (2014). www.betteroregon.org

Executive Office of the President. (2014). 2014 Native youth report. https://obamawhitehouse.archives.gov/sites/default/files/docs/20141129nativeyouthreport_final.pdf

Haberman, M. (2005). Teacher burnout in Black and White. *New Educator, 1*(3), 153–175. https://doi.org.10.1080/15476880590966303

Little, B. (2018). Government boarding schools once separated Native American children from families. https://www.history.com/news/government-boarding-schools-separated-native-american-children-families

Lomawaima, K. T., & McCarty, T. L. (2002). When tribal sovereignty challenges democracy: American Indian education and the democratic ideal. *American Educational Research Journal, 39*(2), 279–305. https://doi.org.10.3102/00028312039002279

"Meriam report: The problem of Indian administration." (1928). https://narf.org/nill/resources/meriam.html

Oregon State Legislature. https://www.oregonlegislature.gov/cis/Pages/minutesAgendas.aspx

Stovall, D. (2004). School leader as negotiator: Critical race theory, praxis, and the creation of productive space. *Multicultural Education, 12*(2), 8–12.

Townsend, J. G. (1938). Disease and the Indian. *Scientific Monthly, 47*(6), 479–495. https://www.jstor.org/stable/16620

U.S. Senate Committee on Labor and Public Welfare. (1969). Indian education: A national tragedy—A national challenge (Kennedy report). https://collegefund.org/

research/indian-education-a-national-tragedy-a-national-challenge-kennedy-report-1969/

Yazzie, E. P. (2003). Missionaries and American Indian languages. https://jan.ucc.nau.edu/~jar/NNL/NNL_14.pdf

*Chapter 8*

# Challenging Leadership to Meet the Needs of Muslim Students in New Zealand

Deborah J. Lomax, Cognition Education Group

### KEY TAKEAWAYS

- Educational leaders need to encourage open dialogue with students, teachers, parents, and members of the school community. There needs to be a shared understanding of the concepts of universal values such as human rights, democracy, secularism, pluralism, tolerance, civility, and cross-cultural and religious morality and values.
- Through shared understanding and acceptance of diversity, a school's curriculum and approach to pedagogy should acknowledge, represent, and strengthen local, national, and global diversity in practice.
- School leaders need to recognize the liberal paradox in secular education systems, find ways to manage this in practice, and teach strategies to support students to manage the tension that arises from this paradox.

[My] teaching philosophy values education as armour in a world conceptually at war. Education protects individuals from becoming cultural dupes. It helps them to make better choices, socially, emotionally and practically (Ablah, 2018).[1]

Access to knowledge is a powerful armory that supports students as they navigate diverse and at times conflicting worldviews in society. In New Zealand, a liberal paradox arises between Muslim communities' right to freedom of religious expression on the one hand and the requirement that we recognize liberal democratic principles in state education and society on the other hand. It is a conflict that arises when individual rights are measured against the "consequence for society as a whole, rather than the consequences for any particular individual or groups in society."[2] The liberal paradox creates challenges for educational leaders when considering whose lens determines what knowledge and pedagogy is valued in education.

This chapter identifies, describes, and explains the challenges faced by Muslim students educated in New Zealand's public schools. Public schools in New Zealand are "owned and funded by the state, and are secular (non-religious)."[3] A small number of state-integrated[4] religious schools are also funded by the government. All state-funded schools are required to deliver a national curriculum that reflects the country's diverse ethnic society and corresponding secular and religious beliefs and values. Consequently there exist challenges for educational leaders when recognizing religious diversity in this secular education system.

School leaders operating in a secular education system are tasked with determining how best to respond to students if they or their family have fundamentally different values and practices than those recognized by the system. In turn, state-integrated school leadership is tasked with responding to a secular education system that may have fundamentally different values and practices than those recognized by their school community. One of the key problems for school leaders is a lack of explicit guidance available to manage the differences between faith-based schooling and secular education.

## INVESTIGATING EDUCATION FOR MUSLIMS IN NEW ZEALAND'S PUBLIC SCHOOLS

Recent research[5] explores the educational experiences of immigrant Muslim students and Muslim and non-Muslim teachers in New Zealand's public schools. Nine research participants shared insights into the ways in which schools regulate, restrict, and reproduce knowledge through their curriculum. Their narratives reveal a tension that they experience, a tension characterized as a liberal paradox. The paradox is apparent in state Muslim schools[6] as they attempt to design a curriculum that aligns their beliefs with the requirements of national curriculum values and principles.

The research reported on in this chapter examines public education set in a culturally defined national identity context. Certain factors affecting identity formation such as culturally pluralistic policies, individual and group rights, and the government's response to the Christchurch Mosque shootings in 2019 are considered. Moreover, participants' reoccurring questioning of Muslim identity in a society with liberal identity policies is discussed. This research challenges educational leaders to question how they will equitably respond to the needs of all students.

## NEW ZEALAND'S EDUCATIONAL LANDSCAPE

The research recognizes that approaches to culturally responsive educational leadership are largely determined by a society's social and educational landscape. New Zealand's education system is framed by national policies actively promoting a bicultural[7] society tolerant of diverse religions and cultures.[8] The secular democratic nature of the education system is intended to reinforce tolerance toward differences and to act as one of society's main integrative mechanism to foster social cohesion (Tearney, 2016).

The government's implementation of culturally responsive educational policies followed a significant increase in New Zealand's ethnic diversity in society beginning in the 1970s (Spoonley, 2015a). New Zealand's Private Schools Conditional Integration Act 1975 recognizes cultural responsivity in education by enabling communities to express diverse philosophical beliefs in government-funded, state-integrated schools. State-integrated schools sign an agreement with the government to design a special character curriculum that must also adhere to New Zealand Curriculum principles and values.[9]

To further nurture a shared collective identity that supports social cohesion, all state-funded schools are required to deliver a community-responsive (i.e., localized) curriculum that aligns with the principles of the New Zealand Curriculum.[10] This poses challenges for school leadership to design a localized curriculum in the absence of explicit guidance to manage the diverse educational values that exist within families and communities and faith-based and secular schools.

The lack of guidance for leadership in New Zealand's Muslim state schools to manage diverse educational values has left students and teachers experiencing considerable tension given the restrictions the Muslim community places on the curriculum. These constraints are often related to a lack of alignment between diverse community interpretations of Islam and the democratic principles of the national curriculum.

Despite the socially just intent of New Zealand's policies, cultural freedom in society has been viewed paradoxically by some as a threat to liberal traditional identities as culturally diverse citizens attempt to negotiate very different moral codes.[11] Kolig (2010) expresses his concern that some Muslims believe New Zealand's democratic national identity is not fully accessible to them, which drives some toward a more extreme fundamentalist Muslim identity. Nonetheless other academics recognize that the response to super-diversity in society is open public dialogue and a renegotiation of national identity and citizenship.[12]

One non-Muslim school leader expressed similar concerns to Kolig (2010), stating that the Muslim school she taught at was "turning inwards [post–Christchurch attack, 2019] . . . Proprietors have met to reinforce the Islamification of the school curriculum . . . No-one, teachers included, is allowed to wear a crucifix or have a Bible displayed on the school grounds . . . And all teachers, including non-Muslims, have been told that they must wear a hijab from 2020."[13] This is concerning given that the Muslim students interviewed in my study spoke of the need to move beyond a fundamentalist approach to Islam, modernize the curriculum, and engage more in wider New Zealand society.

Furthermore, schools in New Zealand are required to deliver a curriculum that supports the development of global citizens with a strong national and cultural identity (see Figure 8.1).[14] To achieve this vision the Ministry of Education funds nationwide, culturally responsive professional development for teachers.[15] This approach is intended to strengthen positive teacher-student relationships, to improve student achievement, and to strengthen cultural identity. Moreover it permits the maintenance of students' cultural heritage and the celebration of hyphenated identities[16] such as that of a Muslim-New Zealander.

## EDUCATION SHAPES IDENTITY

New Zealand's social and educational policies of tolerance and acceptance of religious, cultural, and individual diversity are intended to promote an inclusive and united society. Teachers and school leaders should recognize that students' personal identity provides the norms by which individuals judge themselves, and is the basis of their integrity.[17] In a democratic liberal society, students should be provided with opportunities to develop and express a personal identity that allows them to set their own moral compass based on their personal choices and actions.

In order to support students as they strengthen their cultural identity, educationalists need to understand their own cultural biases and recognize that identity does not exist in a vacuum. Muslim identity for example is "shaped on the one hand by discourses long associated with Islamic ethics and law, and, on the other hand, circumstances extrinsic to this normative tradition that inform the way in which those internal discourses are selectively reconstructed in the face of modern plurality."[18]

The Muslim students interviewed during this research recognize that New Zealand laws provide them with the individual right to choose their education, identity, and engagement in society.[19] Despite these laws, the power dynamics between Muslim students and Muslim parents, school management, and teachers does not always afford students access to those rights. This creates tension for Muslim students who understand their legal rights

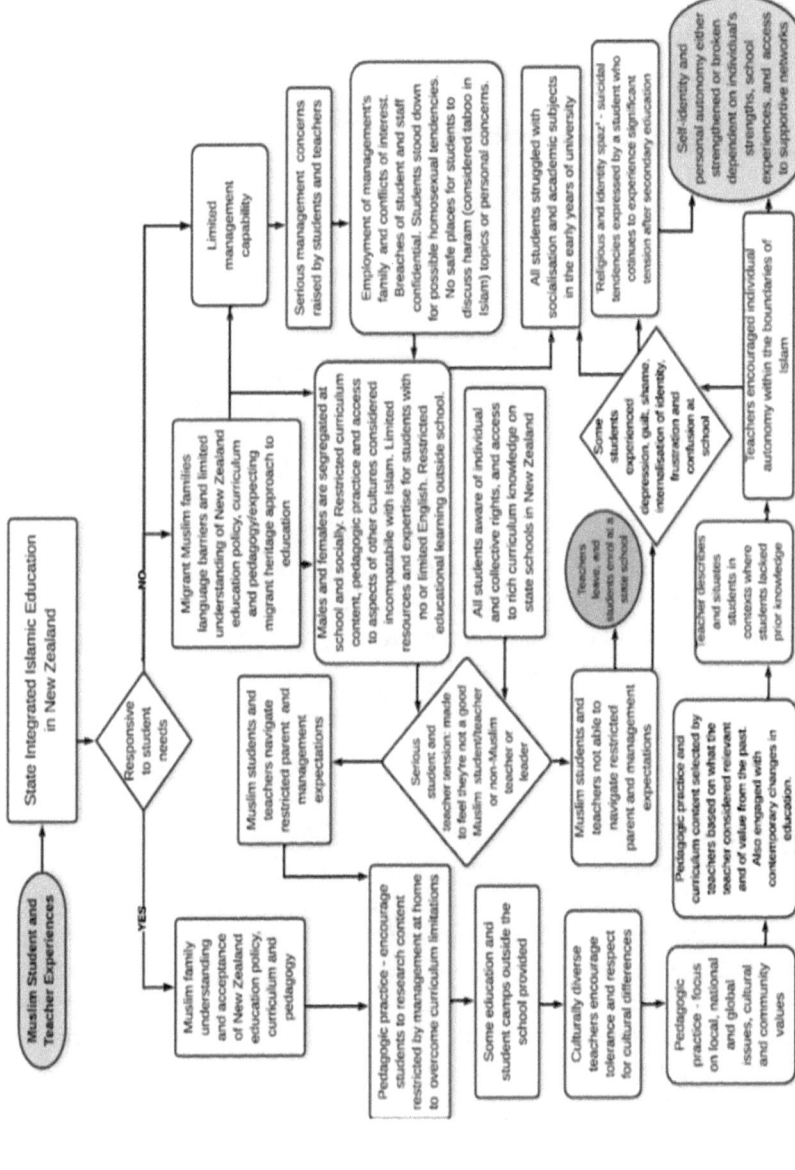

Figure 8.1. State integrated Islamic education in New Zealand.

as New Zealand citizens. State-Muslim school leadership may be concerned with research findings that found some students who experienced overly conservative forms of Islam in schools were deliberately avoiding that approach to Islam in their post-secondary education.

The existential question of Muslim identity in a liberal democratic society was raised by the female students who were interviewed. They discerned that it is not always possible to compromise where opposing faith and secular values exist. They recognized a need to navigate parallel lives to negotiate different and at times irreconcilable moralities to address contradictory religious and liberal values in society.

Jacinda Ardern's[20] decision as a non-Muslim to wear a hijab to address the nation following the Christchurch attack on the Muslim community in 2019 was criticized by some people as a naive representation of Islam.[21] This show of respect for Islam stereotyped female Muslim identity led to reports of some Muslims who previously chose not to wear a hijab being pressured by family members to start wearing one.[22] A non-Muslim wearing a hijab as a symbolic representation of being a Muslim homogenizes their identity and adds to the tension some Muslim females experience in New Zealand and globally.

Pressure to conform to other people's identity ideals is in conflict with an individual's right to choose to wear or not to wear a hijab—in effect their right to determine their personal, religious, and citizenship identity in New Zealand. Policy makers need to recognize that a modern, fluid approach to identity is a further source of tension for some individuals. Educational leaders should consider designing strategies to support students as they navigate this transformative concept of identity.

## MUSLIM STUDENTS' EDUCATIONAL EXPERIENCES

An important aspect of education is recognizing that it is a central institution for the production of identity, for shaping patterns of control, and to legitimate, and in many cases, reproduce, social and cultural norms.[23] Student narratives highlight frustrations with restrictive school policies, a restricted curriculum, and an inability to explore beyond the religious norms taught in state-Muslim schools in New Zealand. Moreover participants shared experiences of being unable to explore identity beyond that which was determined for them at Muslim schools. In contrast, students depicted their secular education as an opportunity to more freely determine the best fit of Islam for their lives.

## STATE-MUSLIM EDUCATION

The greatest source of tension identified by respondents who attended or taught at state-Muslim schools were the diverse community perspectives of Islam and the limited professional capability of some school management and governance. These two key factors restricted the curriculum available to students and constrained any form of identity exploration. Ilham,[24] a Muslim student, shared that she loves "to dance and listen to music, but my religion says no, try to avoid it . . . If I was the principal now, I would let the students participate in those classes, even at the Islamic school." Inability to express identity led to some students being stood-down[25] for perceived displays of homosexual tendencies, creating significant tension for those concerned. As one student explained,

> When they [the state-funded Muslim school staff] . . . asked me if I was gay . . . You can't say "I'm gay." So, I said, no, I'm not . . . studying your religion, your culture, being involved in political talk, opening your mind, whether it's online . . . It doesn't have to be about going to a school that drains you physically, mentally, emotionally and spiritually especially.[26]

This student is at a crossroad in her life, aware of the ability to form and express a personalized identity while at the same time experiencing a breakdown of traditional, cultural, and religious structures that causes stress. Her school's traditionalist approach to Islam in education and the school's inability to support Asmara's increasingly modern sense of identity left her confused and in a "kind of religious spaz."[27] The conservative religious constraints she experienced in education and at home were incongruent with her modern world lens. This ongoing discord left her in a state of depression and experiencing suicidal tendencies.[28]

Asmara, Ilham, and Menaal (Muslim students) had difficulty transitioning to university life in New Zealand. Ilham[29] described being "accustomed to isolating ourselves with other Muslims." They each spoke of the culture shock of university life, having never been in contact with males other than those in their own family. Menaal accepts that the restrictions in her life are driven by her education and her family's beliefs. She also recognizes that New Zealand's laws protect her individual right to choose to adopt her family's beliefs and their corresponding restrictions.

Post-secondary education, Asmara and Ilham remain devout to Islam while choosing to avoid any extreme version of Islam that resembles their experiences at their respective Muslim schools. Experiences that they described would often make them "feel like bad Muslims." Asmara's depiction of "high school as a cage," which left her feeling suicidal, "and university is like being freed," should encourage leadership to urgently review Muslim school policies.

## STATE-SECULAR EDUCATION

Neither Ablah nor Arif (Muslim students) spoke of tension experienced at the secular coeducational schools they attended. Ablah explained that the stresses she experienced were predominantly in the home, in particular when she questioned her parents about their cultural and religious norms that no longer made sense to her in a modern secular society. Nonetheless she also described her family as quite liberal in that "no female in my family, who identify as Muslim, wears [a] hijab—and that is 95% of my family, five generations back. They wear Western clothes."

Ablah's school environment was multi-ethnic with an "extremely high proportion of foreign students." Diversity was positively reinforced at her school, which "encouraged a journey of finding one's place." Her secular life at school and university led to a fragmentation of the traditional structures that had previously defined her identity. Consequently she "struggled to build my identity as a woman . . . [I] wanted to be financially independent. I wanted to choose to marry or not marry. I wanted the opportunity to experience both haram and halal[30] things, and then learn and choose my own path."

She portrayed her secular education as the discovery of new knowledge, her identity, and the collective identity of her family's culture and religion. Moreover Ablah had begun to recognize the potential danger of homogenizing Muslim identity and imposing those views and experiences on others. Unlike the other females interviewed, Ablah easily transitioned to university life. She was also the only female Muslim interviewed who chose to live alone, away from her family before marriage, creating angst in her Muslim community.

An important point to recognize in this research is that the sole male Muslim student participant, Arif, spoke of no restraints imposed on his life either before or after coming to New Zealand. Different expectations placed on females compared to males by their Muslim community, and the higher visibility for those females wearing a hijab, is likely related to their different educational experiences. Arif described growing up at a boarding school in Malaysia without his family influencing his interpretation of Islam. He appreciated that the coeducational secular school he attended had high academic expectations of him and "showed respect for my religion and me" (Arif, 2019).

Arif believes the education he received in New Zealand has strengthened his Muslim identity. He confidently participates in the university basketball team and investment club and lives with Muslim and non-Muslim university students in Christchurch. In his opinion, "after the [Christchurch] shooting incident, people are more aware and accepting of Muslims and we will be able to contribute more in society" (Arif, 2019).

In summary, this research identified that the type of education Muslim students receive affects the level of tension they experience to learn, to self-identify, and to engage in wider society. The evidence supports the assertion that while Muslim students experience various tensions in education, they are finding ways to negotiate these tensions. Students' university experiences appear to have helped them to develop the confidence needed to socialize in wider secular life regardless of the nature of their earlier education. Nevertheless all of the students spoke of a need for Muslim communities to exercise some flexibility of Islam in education in a modern liberal society.

## TEACHERS EDUCATING MUSLIMS IN NEW ZEALAND

In this section I examine what knowledge teachers value in education and their pedagogic characteristics by applying Bernstein's[31] concept of pedagogic identities to their interview responses. Bernstein's pedagogic identities are a representation of teachers' different educational biases toward what is valued knowledge, the approach they take to regulate and manage educational change, their moral lens, and their response to cultural diversity in schools. The investigation of teachers' pedagogic values helps us to analyze the relationship between power and knowledge and the effect this may have on students in education.[32]

### Muslim Teachers

Ablah, an immigrant Muslim teacher at a state-Muslim school, epitomizes on the one hand a liberal Muslim identity with tattoos and multiple ear piercings to boot. Moreover, she chooses to distance herself from any form of Islam that she considers too extreme or conservative. On the other hand, Ablah abhors aspects of New Zealand's liberal society because, she says, "it goes against my moral code." Her responses reflect a pedagogic identity that values traditions that make sense to her in contemporary society while nurturing a future-focused orientation toward education.

Despite Ablah's contrasting liberal-conservative values, she expressed "very little interest in maintaining traditionalism unless it is functional to the context in which she is living." She spoke of encouraging Muslim students "to be the captains of their own ship ... [to] be financially independent" and encouraged students to develop a modern interpretation of Islam, asserting,

Not their culture, or community, or even parents, should force them into a way of life that they do not agree with in their hearts. My mission was to make sure that no foreign woman[33] coming to New Zealand was ever trapped by her culture or . . . her religion again. This is why I went on to become a teacher. So that I can make the experience of being a Muslim or a foreigner in New Zealand an empowering situation—rather than an alien one.

Ablah motivated students to research at home any subject content that might be considered *haram* in the school curriculum. She spoke of students sometimes choosing "very controversial topics and texts that I cannot teach in class . . . [such as] cults, sex-slavery . . . and race politics in New Zealand." By suggesting students research haram content at home, Ablah was removing some of the barriers to knowledge acquisition that some Muslim students face in education. Nonetheless the strength of this approach hinges on parents' approval for their children to access knowledge that the school considers haram.

Wasay's approach to education illustrates his understanding and tolerance of diversity in education to meet the needs of his students. He spoke of valuing traditions, being future focused, and understanding his students. This New Zealand male Muslim convert "feels blessed [to] work in a genuinely diverse [secular] school to support Muslim students who 'are in a context where their values are often vastly different from those of their home, culture or faith.'"

He describes the tension Muslim families experience with education in New Zealand, suggesting that "the vast bulk of the [Muslim] community [in New Zealand] still cling to migrant or heritage identities. These are not in themselves a problem at all (and many kids successfully navigate both) but are often a source of tension or problems within the families they hail from."

Wasay celebrates his students' diverse cultural and religious backgrounds and actively works to develop relationships with them by sharing his own vulnerabilities as a Muslim convert. He spends a lot of time developing curriculum resources that connect to Muslim students' life experiences and beliefs. By incorporating Islamic content in the senior secondary school curriculum, Wasay is able to make Islam visible to non-Muslim students and teachers and to those governing his school.

### Non-Muslim Teachers

Awhireinga, a non-Muslim Māori who teaches at a state-Muslim school, values cultural traditions and a future-oriented approach to education. This teacher proudly acknowledges her Māori indigenous heritage in students' learning experiences. Awhireinga believes her educational values were shaped by her "own school learning experiences, as a Māori.[34] These experiences helped her to reassert the need "to share my culture and language with the students [that] allows the students to share theirs." She integrates her culture and curriculum to help students reflect on their identity and place in New Zealand society. Her approach helps to make Māori culture visible in a Muslim curriculum.

Ratnajyoti, a non-Muslim immigrant, values contemporary change and a future-focused approach to education. She believes "it is vital that our students' value both their religious and cultural heritage as well as their identity as Kiwis [colloquialism for a New Zealander]. Many [Muslim students] are refugees and most are migrants, all of whom have a valuable contribution to make to this country." She expresses concerns with the restrictions placed on access to knowledge at the state-Muslim school where she taught.

Awhireinga and Ratnajyoti spoke of the difficulties they experienced incorporating Islam into their respective subject area at the Muslim schools at which they taught. Ratnajyoti was concerned with changes in the teaching of Islam. She asserted that after the Christchurch tragedy, the school's views were "no longer balanced and [had] become quite fanatical. There has been an onslaught of extreme views of Islam pushed by the principal. It is a concerning way to shape the Muslim students' identity here in New Zealand."

All of the teachers at the state-Muslim schools were prohibited from teaching parts of their specialty curriculum. For example, students were not able to draw faces in art; health was not introduced until students reached year 11 (ages 15–16); and music was not offered. These restrictions meant teachers needed to creatively make the invisible—that is, unknown or otherwise restricted or prohibited knowledge—visible, that is, known to students.[35]

The overall responses from teachers reveal practitioners who value an education focused on local and community issues and culture and identity and is future oriented. These values reflect the professional expectations[36] placed on them to deliver a localized curriculum based on the principles of the New Zealand Curriculum.[37] The teachers all agree students should have access to all knowledge to enable them to choose the person they will be in the future. All of the teachers implement teaching strategies that nurture students' religious and cultural identity.

Only one teacher regarded an individual and global Muslim identity to be more important than a national identity despite having lived in New Zealand for over a decade. This teacher also admitted that she had no idea how she would nurture Muslim students to identify with a New Zealand national identity. The other teachers who were interviewed believed that students should develop hyphenated identities that linked their Muslim identity to the national identity. Furthermore, three of these five teachers were immigrants who self-identified with a hyphenated national identity linked to New Zealand.

## IMPLICATIONS FOR EDUCATIONAL LEADERS

The participants' personal narratives make apparent the tension students and teachers are experiencing in New Zealand's public schools (see Figure 8.2). The students who had been educated at state-Muslim schools experienced considerable anxiety at university when adjusting to a coeducational and secular environment. Interestingly they dealt with this anxiety by dissociating from Muslims who held overly conservative views of Islam. This is a significant finding particularly in light of one Muslim school's shift toward being less tolerant of secularism and more conservative in its approach to education.

Overall the research found that the students who experienced a more moderate approach to Islam at school experienced less tension and felt more confident in their personal identity and in their ability to integrate with wider New Zealand society. Those students who received a stricter religious education experienced considerable tension, were more conflicted in their personal identity, and were more likely to withdraw from overly conservative forms of Islam.

Although the study was small, the findings suggest that Muslim schools are experiencing considerable challenges in the design of a localized Muslim curriculum that also aligns with national curriculum expectations. This tension is the liberal paradox, a condition that on the one hand empowers Muslim communities and on the other hand constrains them[38] in a secular education system.

## REFLECTIVE QUESTIONS

- Whose lens determines what is of value in your school curriculum?
- How would you design a curriculum and pedagogy that is individualized to meet student need and interest if it conflicted with their family's expectations or the expectations outlined in national educational policy?
- What networks are available in the community that could support your school to increase staff knowledge of Islam and to develop cultural competency?
- How can your school work with local communities to support immigrant families to develop cultural competency and language acquisition of their adopted country?

*Challenging Leadership to Meet the Needs of Muslim Students in New Zealand* 107

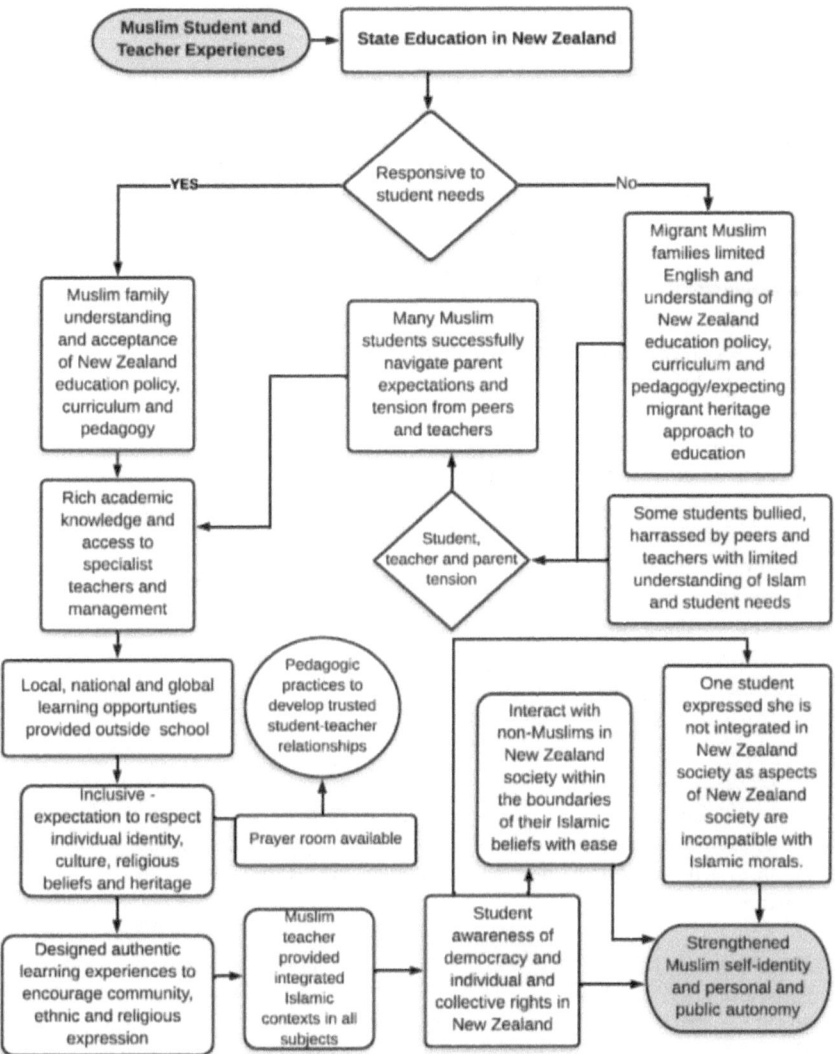

Figure 8.2. State education in New Zealand.

## NOTES

1. Pseudonyms have been used for all of the participant names. Interview dates are referenced with pseudonyms.
2. Codd, 1993, p. 81.
3. New Zealand Ministry of Education, 2021.
4. State-integrated schools were first established in New Zealand under the Private Schools Conditional Integration Act 1975. "State-Muslim school" and

"state-integrated school" are used interchangeably in this chapter to refer to a state-funded Muslim school.

5. Lomax, 2015, 2021; Lomax & Rata, 2016.
6. In New Zealand there are only two state-funded Muslim schools that are located in Auckland where the largest Muslim community resides.
7. These bicultural policies are based on the principles of the Treaty of Waitangi, considered New Zealand's founding document establishing the relationship between the indigenous people, Māori, and the British Crown. In modern New Zealand society, bicultural policies relate to the rights of Māori and all non-Māori.
8. University of Waikato, 2022.
9. New Zealand Ministry of Education, 2007.
10. New Zealand Ministry of Education, 2007.
11. Kolig, 2010.
12. Spoonley, 2015b.
13. Ratnajyoti, 2021.
14. Education New Zealand et al., 2018.
15. University of Waikato, 2022.
16. Ward & Liu, 2012.
17. Parekh, 2008.
18. Hefner, 2014, p. 131.
19. New Zealand Bill of Rights Act, 1990; New Zealand Government, 2019.
20. The current New Zealand prime minister and leader of the Labour Party since 2017.
21. Llewellyn, 2019; Tripathi, 2020.
22. Shakir, 2019.
23. Lewis, 2004, pp. 151–152.
24. Ilham, 2018.
25. A principal (school leader) of a state-funded school can "stand down" (send home from school for up to five days) a student for serious misconduct or continual disobedience.
26. Asmara, 2018.
27. Asmara, 2018.
28. Asmara, 2018, 2019.
29. Ilham, 2018.
30. *Haram* refers to things considered unacceptable in Islam; *halal* refers to things considered acceptable in Islam.
31. Bernstein, 2000.
32. Bernstein, 2003.
33. Ablah's reference to "foreign women" refers to immigrant women.
34. Awhireinga, 2018.
35. Bernstein, 2000, 2003.
36. Teaching Council New Zealand, 2022.
37. New Zealand Ministry of Education, 2017.
38. Berman, 1992, p. 42.

# REFERENCES

Berman, M. (1992). Why modernism still matters. In S. Lash and J. Friedman. (Eds.). *Modernity & identity.* Blackwell.

Bernstein, B. (2000). *Pedagogy, symbolic control and identity: Theory, research, critique* (2nd ed.). Rowman & Littlefield.

Bernstein, B. (2003). *Class, codes and control: Towards a theory of educational transmission.* Routledge.

Codd, J. A. (1993). Equity and choice: The paradox of New Zealand educational reform. *Curriculum Studies, 1*(1), 75–90. https://www.doi.org.10.1080/0965975930010105

Education New Zealand et al., (2018). *International education strategy: He Rautaki Matauranga A Ao 2018–2030.* Wellington, New Zealand. https://enz.govt.nz/assets/Uploads/International-Education-Strategy-2018-2030.pdf

Hefner, R. W. (2014). Modern Muslims and the challenge of plurality. *Society, 51*(2), 131–139. https://doi.org/10.1007/s12115-014-9752-7

Kolig, E. (2010). *New Zealand's Muslims and multiculturalism: Muslim minorities.* Brill.

Lewis, N. (2004). Embedding the reforms in New Zealand schooling: After neo-liberalism? *Geo Journal, 59*(2), 149–160.

LLewellyn, O. (2019). Jacinda Ardern increasingly criticised for her endorsement of female head coverings. https://www.rightminds.nz/articles/jacinda-ardern-increasingly-criticised-her-endorsement-female-headcoverings

Lomax, D. (2015). *Curriculum dilemmas: A study of an Islamic girls' secondary school in New Zealand.* [Unpublished master's thesis]. University of Auckland.

Lomax, D. (2021). *The liberal paradox for Muslims educated in New Zealand.* [Unpublished doctoral thesis]. University of Auckland. https://www.library.auckland.ac.nz/search/provider:theses/The%20Liberal%20paradox%20for%20Muslims%20educated%20in%20New%20Zealand

Lomax, D., and Rata, E. (2016). Diversity, social cohesion and the curriculum: A study of a Muslim girls' secondary school in New Zealand. *Pacific-Asian Education Journal, 28*(1), 31–49.

New Zealand Bill of Rights Act 1990.

New Zealand Government. (2019). Human rights and freedoms. https://www.govt.nz/browse/law-crime-and-justice/human-rights-in-nz/human-rights-and-freedoms/

New Zealand Ministry of Education. (2007). The New Zealand Curriculum. http://nzcurriculum.tki.org.nz/The-New-Zealand-Curriculum

New Zealand Ministry of Education. (2017). The New Zealand Curriculum. https://nzcurriculum.tki.org.nz/The-New-Zealand-Curriculum#collapsible5

New Zealand Ministry of Education. (2021). Education in New Zealand. https://www.education.govt.nz/our-work/our-role-and-our-people/education-in-nz/

Parekh, B. (2005). *Rethinking multiculturalism: Cultural diversity and political theory.* Red Globe Press.

Parekh, B. (2008). *A new politics of identity: Political principles for an interdependent world.* Red Globe Press.

Private Schools Conditional Integration Act 1975.

Shakir, A. (2019). Don't let Jacinda Ardern's headscarf send the wrong message. Stuff. https://www.stuff.co.nz/national/christchurch-shooting/116195738/dont-let-jacinda-arderns-headscarf-send-the-wrong-message

Simon-Kumar, R. (2019). *The multicultural dilemma: Amid rising diversity and unsettled equity issues, New Zealand seeks to address its past and present.* https://www.migrationpolicy.org/article/rising-diversity-and-unsettled-equity-issues-new-zealand

Spoonley, P. (2015a). New diversity, old anxieties in New Zealand: The complex identity politics and engagement of a settler society. *Ethnic and Racial Studies, 38*(4), 650–661.

Spoonley, P. (2015b). "I made a space for you": Renegotiating national identity and citizenship in contemporary alternate or New Zealand. In G. Ghosh & J. Leckie (Eds.). *Asians and the new multiculturalism in Aotearoa New Zealand.* Otago University Press.

Teaching Council New Zealand. (2022). Our code our standards. https://teachingcouncil.nz/professional-practice/our-code-our-standards/#:~:text=The%20Code%20sets%20out%20the,expectations%20of%20effective%20teaching%20practice

Tearney, F. (2016). History of education in New Zealand. http://www.mcguinnessinstitute.org/wp-content/uploads/2016/08/20161213-Working-Paper-2016%EF%80%A203-History-of-education-in-New-Zealand.pdf

Tripathi, N. (2020). *Muslim campaigners slam New Zealand women for wearing hijab in solidarity: "The hijab is not empowering."* https://meaww.com/muslim-women-campaigners-slam-new-zealand-women-for-wearing-headscarf-say-hijab-not-empowering

University of Waikato. (2022). Poutama Pounamu. https://poutamapounamu.org.nz/service

Ward, C., and Liu, J. (2012). Ethno-cultural conflict in Aotearoa: Balancing indigenous rights and multicultural responsibilities. In D. Landis & R. Albert (Eds.). *Handbook of ethnic conflict.* Victoria University of Wellington.

# Index

access, xii, xiv, 16, 20, 44, 49, 53, 54, 55, 61, 91, 92, 95
accountability, 53, 55, 58, 63, 89
Advanced Placement, 16, 58
affinity groups, 49, 52, 53, 59, 61
alternative education, 52, 54, 59, 60
attendance, 19, 63, 83, 89, 90

Black/African American students, vii, xi, xii, xv, 20, 60

California, xii, 50
career and technical education (CTE), 58, 62
certification/licensure, xii, 52, 83, 92
charter schools: intentionally diverse charter schools, 2; no-excuses charter schools, 6
childhood experiences, ix, 50, 84, 85, 86
collaboration, 16, 17, 22, 56, 57, 58, 60, 61, 71, 72, 77, 79, 80, 88, 91
college and career readiness, xi, 18, 20, 55, 58, 59, 89
Colorado, xii
community, 15, 18, 19, 20, 21, 22, 23, 24, 49, 50, 52, 53, 54, 56, 57, 60, 61, 62, 64, 83, 84, 87, 89, 91
COVID-19, 40, 56
critical self-awareness, xxi, 41, 42

cultural responsiveness, viii, xi, xii, xiii, xiv, xv, 16, 18, 89, 91
curriculum, xiv, 19, 53, 62, 82, 89; culturally relevant materials, 19, 53, 62

data use, 58, 60, 63, 64, 89
decision-making, 17, 18, 23, 39, 41, 42, 56, 59, 60, 63
diversity, xi, xii, 43, 51

English learners (ELs)/English language learners (ELLs), 16, 18, 50, 51, 54; English as a new language (ENL), 67, 68, 70, 80
equity, ix, x, xi, xii, xiii, xiv, xv, 15, 16, 17, 18, 20, 23, 49, 50, 53, 54, 55, 56, 59, 60, 62, 64, 65, 83, 86, 88, 89; equity audits, 25–37

family engagement, 20, 54, 56

graduation rates, 59, 60, 63, 89

heritage language, xiv, 16, 84, 91
hiring, viii, 15, 23, 52, 56, 57, 61
historically Black college and university (HBCU), 3, 12

inclusion, 18, 20, 23, 30, 49, 53, 55, 67–82, 88
Indigenous populations, xi, xiii, xiv, xv, 19, 83, 84, 86–92
instructional teams, 68, 70, 77–79
International Baccalaureate Program (IBP), 34, 58

leadership, viii, ix, x, xiii, xv, 15–18, 55, 60, 61, 69–71, 79, 80, 87, 92, 96, 97, 100, 102; education leaders, vii, ix, x, xi, xiii, xiv, 1, 18, 19, 20, 26, 40, 52, 55, 60, 87, 90; instructional leadership, 58, 61, 62; leadership mechanisms, 2, 7–11; leadership motivations, 2, 3–7; leadership pathways, 2, 3; leadership training/certification, 11–12

mentorship, ix, 9–10, 20, 51, 59, 61
migrants, 8, 50, 65, 104
mindfulness, 40, 41, 45
mission statements, 2, 18, 86, 87
Muslim students, 95–110

Native American students, xiv, xv, 19, 83–94
New York, ix, xii, xiv, 2, 25–37
New Zealand, ix, xi, xiii, xiv, xv, 95–110

opportunity gaps, 1, 11, 26, 27, 30
Oregon, x, xii-xiv, xvi, 16, 18, 20, 50, 51, 52, 56, 58, 83, 84, 87–91

parochial schools, xiv, 19, 84
personal narratives, viii, xiv, xv, 50, 65, 92
policy/education policy, x, xi, xii, xiii, xiv, 52, 83–92; policy implementation, xii, xiii, xiv, 17, 18, 19, 40, 45, 56, 57, 88, 89, 90, 91

professional development, 16, 40, 43, 44, 46, 55, 57, 89, 90
professional networks, 10–11

recruitment, xi, xii, xiii, 34, 49, 58, 59, 61, 65
research practice partnership, 26

scheduling, 58, 61, 62, 63, 67–82
service delivery, 29, 67–82
service maps, 67–82
sense of belonging, x, xiv, 19, 39, 40, 42, 43, 44, 45, 47, 49, 53, 55
social justice, viii, ix, 1–14, 25–37, 67–82, 89, 91
special education/students with disabilities, 25–37, 54, 60, 63, 67–82
staffing, xii, 17, 19–23, 40–41, 44, 46, 49, 51 52, 53, 55–56, 67–82; BIPOC leaders/leaders of color, xi, xiii, 52, 60, 61, 65; underrepresented leaders, xii, 20, 49, 52, 53; underrepresented leaders, retention of, viii, xi, 61
student advisory groups, 49, 54
student discipline, xi, 40, 41, 42, 44, 45, 51, 59, 60, 62, 63
systems change, xv, 15, 18, 52, 55, 56, 57, 64, 83, 86, 89

Teach for America (TFA), 5
technology, x, xiv, 39–47, 54; virtual reality (VR), x, xiv, 39–47

unconscious bias, x, xii, 39–47, 52
urban schools, 2, 7, 16, 87

voice: community voice, 15, 18–20, 83, 89; native voice, 87; student voice, 49, 55, 65; teacher voice, 18

Washington State, x, xiii, 50

# Contributors

**Christine Ashby, PhD,** is a professor of inclusive special education and disability studies at Syracuse University. She is also director of the Center on Disability and Inclusion. Professor Ashby's work seeks to disrupt dominant notions of disability as deficiency and underscores the importance of considering the lived experiences of individuals with disabilities and creating contexts for competence in inclusive schools and communities. Her work has been published in such journals as *Equity and Excellence in Education*; *International Journal of Inclusive Education*; *Disability and Society*; *Teacher Education and Special Education*; and *Intellectual and Developmental Disability*.

**Gustavo Balderas, EdD,** is superintendent of the Beaverton School District in Oregon, the third largest school system in the state. He has been a superintendent in Oregon, Washington, and California school systems. He began his life as the child of migrant farm workers in Eastern Oregon and developed his love of learning and passion for education in Oregon Public Schools. He has been an educator for thirty-three years. His career highlights include improving equity through a systems approach in the districts he has led. He has been named Oregon Distinguished Latinx Educator of the Year, Oregon Superintendent of the Year, and AASA National Superintendent of the Year. He is the current president of the national Association of Latino Administrators and Superintendents.

**Meredith Devennie, PhD,** is a fifth-grade teacher in the Liverpool Central School District. She holds a PhD in teaching and curriculum from Syracuse University.

**Rory Edwards** is supervisor of fine art in the Syracuse City School District.

**Nate Franz** is assistant superintendent of curriculum, instruction, and equity in the Jamesville-DeWitt School District. He was formerly assistant superintendent for teaching and learning, supervisor of mathematics, and district math coach in the Syracuse City School District. In addition he worked as a teacher and instructional coach in Washington, DC. He holds an MA in elementary education from American University and a certificate of advanced study in educational leadership and administration from Syracuse University.

**Sarah Gentile** is director of fine arts and coordinator of diversity, equity, and inclusion in the West Genesee Central School District. Previously she was supervisor of fine arts and a music teacher in the Syracuse City School District. She is currently a doctoral candidate in educational leadership at Syracuse University.

**Mona Halcomb** is an enrolled citizen of the Confederated Tribes of the Umatilla Indian Reservation (CTUIR). Currently, she is the Native Student Success Program Supervisor in the Office of Native Education at the Washington Office of Superintendent of Public Instruction (OSPI). She earned both her Bachelor of Arts (Interdisciplinary Studies: Society, Ethics, and Human Behavior) and her Master of Arts in Cultural Studies, with a focus on the Native American Opportunity Gap, from the University of Washington, Bothell. She is completing her Ed.D. June 2023, at the University of Washington, Tacoma. Prior to joining OSPI she served as the Oregon Department of Education's Indian Education Specialist. Working closely with State agencies, Tribes, native communities, and organizations to close the opportunity gap for American Indian/Alaska Native students and youth, Mona has served as the education director for her tribe and worked in both two-and-four-year higher education institutions to support students' academic pursuits.

**Decoteau Irby, PhD,** is an associate professor in the Department of Educational Policy Studies at the University of Illinois, Chicago. He researches equity-focused school leadership as a lever to improve Black children's academic and socio-emotional experiences and outcomes. He holds a PhD in urban education from Temple University.

**Kimana Kibriani** is a doctoral candidate in educational leadership at Syracuse University. She holds an MA in public administration from Binghamton University. Previously she was lecturer and coordinator at Shanto Marium University and elected vice-chair of a subdistrict in a local government tier in her native Bangladesh.

**Elisabeth Kim, PhD,** is an assistant professor of education and leadership at California State University, Monterey Bay. Previously she was a Robert Curvin Postdoctoral Associate at the Joseph C. Cornwall Center for Metropolitan Studies at Rutgers University, Newark. She holds a PhD in education policy from Teachers College, Columbia University. Her research uses a mixed-methods approach to explore the links between education policy and educational equity with a particular focus on how contemporary policies moderate or exacerbate inequities for low-income students of color. Her research interests include culturally responsive and sustaining education, student discipline policy, and urban education reform.

**Sarah Lent, PhD,** is academic staff at the Wisconsin Center of Education Research (WCER) and teaches in the Rehabilitation Psychology and Special Education department at the University of Wisconsin-Madison. Sarah has over ten years of experience in special education, both as a classroom teacher and administrator in Chicago, IL and Brooklyn, NY. She holds her PhD in Educational Leadership and Policy Analysis from University of Wiscon sin-Madison.

**Deborah Lomax, PhD,** is Auckland Regional Manager for the Cognition Education Group, where she manages a team of Professional Learning Development consultants. Previously, Deborah led Ministry of Education-funded responses to the Covid-19 crisis to bring students back into education and nationally led Learning Support and Local Curriculum Design. Her PhD from the University of Auckland's School of Critical Studies in Education explored the educational experiences of immigrant Muslim students as well as Muslim and non-Muslim teachers in New Zealand's public schools and was nominated for the Vice Chancellor's Best Doctorate award in 2021.

**Heather McClure, PhD,** is director of the Center for Equity Promotion at the University of Oregon's College of Education where she also serves as a research assistant professor. She is a broadly trained prevention scientist with expertise in the social and cultural determinants of learning and health among marginalized populations with a particular focus on Latinx immigrant youth and families. She uses multi-method approaches to gain insights into individual-, family-, and community-level influences on learning and critically related phenomena that can either create risk for educational failure or promote engaged learning and well-being over the course of a lifetime.

**Wendy Morgan** is CEO and founder of SHIFT. Wendy is a lifelong educator and a diversity, equity, and inclusion expert driven by a passion for seeing equity and inclusion become bedrock values in her community and society. She has over 20 years of experience in training and in designing innovative education platforms.

**Jo Smith, PhD,** is a Senior Lecturer in education policy and leadership in the University of Auckland's Faculty of Education and Social Work. Her research is situated at the intersection of policy and practice and examines the governance structures that both hinder and help schools and school systems enact reforms aimed at improving outcomes for all students. She is currently embarking on research to increase empathy and dismantle bias through the use of virtual reality.

**Ben Steuerwalt** is director of physical education, health and athletics in the Syracuse City School District. Previously he was a physical education teacher and wellness coordinator in the district. He holds a master's degree in physical education from State University of New York, Cortland.

**George Theoharis, PhD,** is a professor of teaching and leadership at Syracuse University. He has experience as a school principal and teacher and at Syracuse University has served as department chair, associate dean for urban partnerships, and director of field relations. His work preparing leaders and teachers as well as partnering with schools focuses on issues of equity, justice, diversity, inclusion, and school reform and bridges the worlds of K–12 schools and higher education. His most recent books are *Five Practices for Equity Focused School Leadership*; *Parenting in the Pandemic: The Collision of School, Work, and Life at Home*; and *Leadership for Increasingly Diverse Schools*.

**Iton Udosenata, EdD,** is assistant superintendent at Salem-Keizer Public Schools, Oregon. Udosenata has dedicated his career to working to promote equity, social justice, and college-and-career readiness. He earned a BA in ethnic studies, an MA in education leadership, and a PhD in educational leadership at the University of Oregon. He was selected as a Broad Fellow for the 2022–2023 Fellowship for Public Education Leadership, an executive leadership program at Yale School of Management. He served as president of the Coalition of Oregon School Administrators from 2019–2022.

**Corey Williams, PhD,** is a senior data analyst for Student Support Services in the Syracuse City School District. He holds an MA in public administration from Syracuse University.

www.ingramcontent.com/pod-product-compliance
Lightning Source LLC
Chambersburg PA
CBHW032048300426
44117CB00009B/1237